Where to From Here?

A guide for individuals working
the Twelve Steps
of RSA

BlackHawk Canyon
PUBLISHERS

22772 Centre Drive, Suite 205
Lake Forest, CA 92630

COPYRIGHT NOTICE

© 2011 by BlackHawk Canyon Publishers

2 3 4 5 6 7 8 9 10

All rights reserved. No part of this work may be reproduced or transmitted in any form by any means without express, written consent from the publisher.

The author and publisher have taken care in the preparation of this work, but make no expressed or implied warranty of any kind and assume no responsibility for errors or omissions. No liability is assumed for incidental or consequential damages in connection with, or arising out of the use of the information or exercises contained herein.

The characters presented in this work are composite fictions, representing true stories from multiple individuals. The stories have been modified to protect the anonymity of all persons. Any resemblance to any specific person, living or dead, is coincidental.

BlackHawk Canyon Publishers
22772 Centre Dr., Suite 205
Lake Forest, CA 92630

Scripture taken from HOLY BIBLE, NEW INTERNATIONAL VERSION. © Copyright 1973, 1978, 1984 International Bible Society. Used by permission of Zondervan Bible Publishers.

Title: Where to from here? A guide for individuals working the twelve steps of RSA.

self-help, psychology, sexual addiction, recovery, religion, spirituality, step study

---

The Twelve Steps and Twelve Traditions of Alcoholics Anonymous have been reprinted and adapted with the permission of Alcoholics Anonymous World Services, Inc. ("A.A.W.S."). Permission to reprint and adapt the Twelve Steps and Twelve Traditions does not mean that Alcoholics Anonymous is affiliated with this program. A.A. is a program of recovery from alcoholism only – use of A.A.'s Steps and Traditions or an adapted version of its Steps and Traditions in connection with programs and activities which are patterned after A.A., but which address other problems, or use in any other non-A.A. context, does not imply otherwise. Additionally, while A.A. is a spiritual program, A.A. is not a religious program. Thus, A.A. is not affiliated with any sect, denomination, or specific religious belief.

The Serenity Prayer

God, grant me the serenity
to accept the things I cannot change;
the courage to change the things I can;
and the wisdom to know the difference.

Living one day at a time;
Enjoying one moment at a time;
Accepting hardships as the pathway to peace;
Taking, as He did, this sinful world
as it is, not as I would have it;
Trusting that He will make all things right
if I surrender to His Will;
That I may be reasonably happy in this life
and supremely happy with Him
Forever in the next.
Amen.

— Reinhold Niebuhr

Table of Contents

The Serenity Prayer v
The Twelve Steps of RSA ix
The Twelve Traditions of RSA xi
Acknowledgements xiii
About Renewed Hope/RSA Ministries xiv
Introduction xv

Step One 19
    Powerlessness 20
    Preoccupation 21
    Tolerance 24
    Loss of Control 27
    Sexual Behavior History 31
    Addiction History Timeline 31
    Genogram 36

Step Two 39
    Came to Believe 40
    That God 41
    Does God Exist? 42
    General Revelation 43
    Special Revelation 45
    Who is God to You? 46
    Could Restore Us To Sanity 47

Step Three 51
    Dr. Jekyll & Mr. Hyde 52
    Faith 53
    Who is Jesus? 53
    Restored to Sanity 55
    Finding Bottom 55
    Surrender 56
    Temptation 57
    Satan's Lies 58
    God's Truth 60
    Repentance 61
    A Daily Walk 63

Step Four 65
    Morality 66
    Resentments 67
    Freedom 69
    Fears 70

Sexual Relations	71
Repentance	72
A Fearless Moral Inventory	73
Character	75

Step Five 77
    Admitted to God 78
    To Ourselves 80
    And to Another 80
    The Exact Nature 81
    Fifth Step Guidelines 81

Step Six 85
    Were Entirely Willing 85
    To Have God Remove 87
    Our Defects of Character 88
    Willing to be Willing 89
    Character Surgery 91
    Change 92
    Defects into Assets 93
    Prayer Journal 93

Step Seven 97
    Humbly 97
    Asked Him 99
    To Remove 101
    Our Shortcomings 103
    Prayer Journal 106

Step Eight 109
    Responsibility 111
    Repentance 113
    Commitment 114
    Repentance Worksheet 115
    Made a List 117
    And Became Willing 117
    To Make Amends 118
    To Them All 119
    Amends Preparation Worksheet 121

Step Nine 123
    Made Direct Amends 123
    Amends vs Apologies 125
    Respect 126
    Wherever Possible 126
    Except 127

    Systems Check 132
    Peace 134

Step Ten 137
    Personal Inventory 138
    Why Take Inventory? 139
    Stinkin' Thinkin' 140
    When We Were Wrong 141
    Promptly Admitted 142
    A Daily Inventory 143

Step Eleven 157
    Sought 159
    Through Prayer 159
    To Improve 161
    Praying for Knowledge 161
    And the Power 163
    Spirituality Calendar 166

Step Twelve 169
    Having Had An Awakening 170
    As A Result of these Steps 170
    Tried To Carry This Message 173
    To Other Lust Addicts 177
    To Practice These Principles 178
    In All Our Affairs 178

Bibliography 181

The Twelve Steps
Of RSA

1. We admitted we were powerless over lust – that our lives had become unmanageable.

2. Came to believe that God could restore us to sanity.

3. Made a decision to turn our will and our lives over to the care of God.

4. Made a searching and fearless moral inventory of ourselves.

5. Admitted to God, to ourselves and to another human being the exact nature of our wrongs.

6. Were entirely ready to have God remove all these defects of character.

7. Humbly asked Him to remove our shortcomings.

8. Made a list of all persons we had harmed, and became willing to make amends to them all.

9. Made direct amends to such people wherever possible, except when to do so would injure them or others.

10. Continued to take personal inventory and when we were wrong promptly admitted it.

11. Sought through prayer and meditation to improve our relationship with God praying for knowledge of His will for us, and the power to carry that out.

12. Having had a spiritual awakening as the result of these steps, we tried to carry this message to other lust addicts, and to practice these principles in all our affairs.

The Twelve Traditions of RSA

1. Our common welfare should come first; personal recovery depends upon RSA unity.

2. For our group purpose there is but one ultimate authority — a loving God as He may express Himself in our group conscience. Our leaders are but trusted servants; they do not govern.

3. The only requirement for RSA membership is a desire to stop lusting.

4. Each group should be autonomous except in matters affecting other groups or RSA as a whole.

5. Each group has but one primary purpose—to carry its message to the lustaholic who still suffers.

6. An RSA group ought never endorse, finance or lend the RSA name to any related facility or outside enterprise, lest problems of money, property and prestige divert us from our primary purpose.

7. Every RSA group ought to be fully self-supporting, declining outside contributions. Each group should contribute periodically to the national office to support RSA's efforts to bring the Good News of recovery to those who still struggle.

8. RSA should remain forever nonprofessional, but our service centers may employ special workers.

9. RSA, as such, ought never be organized; but we may create service boards or committees directly responsible to those they serve.

10. RSA has no opinion on outside issues; hence the RSA name ought never be drawn into public controversy.

11. Our public relations policy is based on attraction rather than promotion; we need always maintain personal anonymity at the level of press, radio, internet and films.

12. Anonymity is the spiritual foundation of all our traditions, ever reminding us to place principles before personalities.

Acknowledgements

This work is dedicated to those who came before us, who shared of their experience, hope and wisdom to show us the path of recovery, and to those who have yet to find the path. I would like to express my sincere gratitude to the many people in various recovery rooms and to my patients, all of whom continue to teach me every day.

I give any credit that may come due this work to Our Lord and Savior, Jesus of Nazareth. For it is not of my own wisdom, but His. I have the easy job, I hold the pen, and He dictates.

I thank those who have believed in the importance of this work and who encouraged, guided, and supported me. There is a group of men who have been my friends since high school and now serve as the Board of Directors for Renewed Hope. I would have folded up my little tent and gone home long ago were it not for their continual prodding and oversight: Kenneth Cook, Barn Cochran, Chris Hoffman, and Don Palmer. I also owe an immeasurable debt of gratitude to my mentor, Mal McSwain. I am one of many, many people who owe this humble and wise man the certainty of the knowledge of our salvation. Thanks guys, to all of you, and to your wives and families, for believing in the vision our Lord gave me, and in my ability to steward it well. Also, I thank my good friends David Zailer and Mark Laaser, for their continual support, encouragement, and guidance. Finally, and most importantly, I want to acknowledge the support and encouragement of my best friend and partner in this life, my wife, Shari.

About Renewed Hope and RSA Ministries

Renewed Hope is a 501 (C) 3, Federally exempt, non-profit corporation whose mission is to produce Christ-centered, 12 step programs and materials for those who struggle with compulsive sexual behaviors and for those who love them. Renewal from Sexual Addiction (RSA) Ministries is our "public face", or the name used for our face-to-face meetings and our online sober recovery community. We have face-to-face meetings in multiple states in the U.S. plus a meeting in Canada.

We believe that the cornerstone for our recovery is the power, grace, and love of Jesus Christ. The rest of our recovery "house" is built upon; the fellowship of the group, having a safe place to share our struggles, pain, and victories, the accountability of the group, and the mutual support of group members throughout the week.

Our program materials include all of the structure needed to start and run three different types of traditional participation meetings: 1) for men, 2) for women who struggle with sexual addiction, and 3) for spouses of sexually addicted individuals. The addition of the "Where To From Here?" step study guides provides a much needed structure for those desiring more in-depth step work. If you are interested in starting an RSA meeting in your area, or if you are in an existing meeting that would like to adopt the RSA format, please contact us via our website (www.rsaministries.org).

The first RSA meeting was held in 1993 and was a men's participation meeting held on the campus of Saddleback Valley Community Church. A group of 24 brave souls walked into the room on that first night and began their journey of sobriety. In 1995 we released our materials for the first Christ-centered program for spouses, and we called it, "Renewal from Co-Sexual Addiction", or "R-CoSA". Committed to working their own program and finding the love they need through their relationship with Christ instead of through their husbands, these courageous women chose to let go of the insanity of attempting to control uncontrollable people, places, and things, and let God control their lives. Later, in 1997, the first RSA meeting for women was started and called, "RSA-W," or Renewal from Sexual Addiction for Women. This meeting is unique in the world as it provides a safe haven for women with compulsive sexual behaviors to gather to share in their strength, hope, and wisdom and seek recovery through their relationship with Christ Jesus. Finally, in 1999 the first RSA Step Study meeting was held, and we began the process of developing the step study guide materials that you hold in your hand today.

If you are not yet a member of RSA, please feel free to join our online sober community at www.rsaministries.org. There you will find a number of resources to help you attain and maintain your recovery. Join us, won't you, and share of your strength and hope in Christ, or borrow some of ours.

Introduction

Recovering from a life that has been centered on compulsive sexual behaviors is a daunting task for any one. It is a challenge best accepted when you are well prepared and surrounded by supportive people who love you. As a rule, we recommend that step work begin after a person has attained a year of sobriety or more, has a good relationship with a sponsor, and has multiple accountability partners. Due to the nature of step work, it is more likely to threaten one's sobriety than it is to strengthen it.

When many of us arrived at program we were neck-deep in chaos. We had made a complete mess of our lives and had ruined our relationships with families, friends, and others. Some of us had even lost jobs due to our addiction or suffered other financial losses. Some of us had ruined our health. Our lives had become "unmanageable," or as one member put it, "A wrecked train looking for a place to park." We were directed to a place of recovery, where others with similar problems talked about where they had been, what their life was like then, and what it is like now.

We kept coming back, week after week. In time, the chaos that had been our lives began to calm down. We learned to listen to those who had walked this path before us, and we began to find recovery. We found a new relationship with our spirituality, and our sobriety began to grow. However, with all of our history behind us, and so much living yet ahead of us, we found ourselves asking our fellow travelers, "Ok. Where to from here?" That is when we learned about "working the steps." They told us that "step work" is the heart of the program and the tool that God will use to help us attain and maintain sobriety.

As you begin this journey of personal character growth, make sure that you have as much sobriety, support, and spiritual growth as you are able to manage. You will need every bit of it. Through the step work, you will face the people, places and things that lined the road you traveled from where you began, to where you are now. Take your time walking this road. Many of us take as much as a year, or more, to complete the twelve steps. Since you will be working the steps many times in the years ahead, there is no rush to finish. Take heart! The path gets easier, and brighter each time you finish it.

Take the time to open each of your step study sessions with prayer. Ask the Lord to open your eyes to see, and your heart to hear the truths about yourself that He wants you to address. Make sure that as many people as possible know about your endeavors, and are praying for you as well. Also, if you are not able to work the steps in a group format, make sure you maintain regular attendance at your meetings, and keep close and frequent communication with your sponsor and accountability partners. May Our Lord and Savior, Jesus Christ, guide you and comfort you as you walk along this road to recovery.

Blessings,

Laird

Rev., Dr. Laird Bridgman
Founder, Renewed Hope and RSA Ministries

The LORD is my shepherd, I shall not be in want.
He makes me lie down in green pastures,
He leads me beside quiet waters,
He restores my soul.
He guides me in paths of righteousness for His name's sake.

Even though I walk through the valley of the shadow of death,
I will fear no evil, for you are with me;
your rod and your staff, they comfort me.
You prepare a table before me in the presence of my enemies.
You anoint my head with oil; my cup overflows.
Surely goodness and love will follow me all the days of my life,
and I will dwell in the house of the LORD forever.

— Psalms 23:1-6 (NIV)

Trust in the LORD
with all your heart
and lean not on your own understanding;
in all your ways acknowledge him,
and He will direct your paths.

— Proverbs 3:5-6

Step One

"We admitted we were powerless over our lust and that our lives had become unmanageable"

> "To suppose that man has a power independent of God, is to suppose that God's power does not extend to all things, i.e., is not infinite."
>
> — David Hartley

Bob hung the phone up on his desk and stared at the clock. "4:30", the clock stared back at him. "I can't believe it, will this day never end?!" Bob grumbled to himself. He shifted in his seat and turned towards his computer monitor. "Ok, Bob, back to the report." After only a few minutes he was still struggling to keep his thoughts on his work. Images of his last visit to the strip club across town kept intruding into his mind. The dancer who called herself "Candy" was vividly distracting him from his report. Candy. Report. Candy. Report. It was like someone else had a remote control and kept changing his mental screen back to Candy every time he tried to focus on his report. "4:40" said the clock. Report. Candy. Report. Candy, Candy, Candy! Bob began plotting his early escape from work. "I'll head to the restroom, and if nobody is in the back hall, I'll go out the back door. Nobody will miss me if I leave now anyway." Bob's plan worked to perfection and in a manner of minutes he was in his car and heading across town.

There is a difference between "doing" a first step and "working" a first step. "Doing" a first step is what happened for almost all of us when we first came to the program. We reached a place in our lives where we were able to see and accept that our sexual behaviors were out of control. One day we heard someone say that they were "powerless" over their lust, and that their life had become unmanageable. Intuitively, we understood that this was true for our life as well. Therefore, we "did" our first step: We admitted to ourselves that we were powerless to control our lust. Finally, we understood the fact that we were powerless. However, we had yet to understand the meaning of powerlessness in our own life. Working the First Step helps us gain this understanding. It is the "first" step towards honesty with ourselves about ourselves.

For the majority of us, the concept of "powerlessness" is difficult to comprehend. Is it possible to be powerless over lust? Could your life really be so affected by lust that it is "unmanageable?" The answer for all of us has been a resounding "Yes!" to both questions. Until we came to grips with those truths, we were unable to find or keep sobriety.

"Powerless" and "unmanageable" are two closely related concepts. Powerless refers to our inability to control our lust. Unmanageable refers to the outcome of a life out-of-control. Because we lack the ability to control our lust, it controls us. It shapes our choices and decisions, and causes us to choose itself over other more important things in our lives. This causes us to neglect our families, or friends, our bodies, our God, and our own interests. Increasingly, our lives show the wear and tear of our neglect. At some point it all falls apart around us, and we begin to realize how out of control we were.

There are three sections to this chapter which are designed to help us realize how we came to be powerless: *Development of Powerlessness*, *Sexual Behavior History*, and *Family Context for Our Addiction*. In each of the three sections use the included questions as tools to help you complete your First Step, but do not limit yourself to using just these questions. You will need plenty of paper and a good pen or pencil. You will also need to have a quiet place to write, and several blocks of uninterrupted time. The odds are, you will not be able to complete all of the exercises in one sitting, and it is best to think of your work as a series of conversations with yourself, instead of a single paper to be written. As addicts, we tend to move in the extremes of life. We go "all out," or do everything all at once. Use this exercise as an opportunity to practice patience and restraint.

Powerlessness

> *"A power over a man's subsistence amounts to a power over his will."*
>
> *— Alexander Hamilton*

Powerless is another word for dependent. At some point, we became dependent on lust to cope with our feelings, life experiences, or some combination of the two. When we were hurt, angry, resentful, lonely, or tired, we turned to lust to take away our negative emotions. Sometimes, when we were particularly happy due to some success, we "celebrated" with a "treat" for ourselves. Whatever the reason, the reality is that we turned to lust instead of a friend, a spouse, a mentor, or God.

Some of us still protested, wondering how someone could be dependent upon lust. In recovery we came to understand that lust is not sexual in nature, it is spiritual. Obviously, it is possible to lust over specific people, bodies, or even just specific parts of bodies. However, we can also lust after cars, boats, jobs, houses, money, or just about anything. In this program, we have also learned that lust is no respecter of age, gender, body shape, socio-economic status, or anything else. Therefore, we learned that lust is not about sex, it is about power... a power to fill a void inside of us that continually empties itself, and thus is insatiable. God is the only power that is able to fill that void.

In God's perspective, being dependent upon something other than Himself is a sin. He calls it by the name, "idolatry." Idolatry is described as "worshipping a false god." You could consider many of our sexual behaviors "worshipful" acts at the feet of a false god. However, idolatry is also the act of giving anything other than God the central place in our lives. In allowing lust to have more and more power in our lives, allowing it to take our time, our energy, our interest and our money, we have allowed it to become THE most important thing in our lives... our "god." Either way, idolatry is idolatry.

There are three 'Red Flags' that are indicators of dependence: 1) a growing preoccupation, 2) a growing tolerance, and 3) a loss of control. In order to comprehend our powerlessness over this disease, we have to understand that it progresses slowly and insidiously. Seeing the progression of the disease and its impact across a lifetime serves as a powerful testimony to the reality that this addiction is much more powerful than any of us. Before we found recovery, we believed that we were in control; now we understand that the tail was truly "wagging the dog."

Preoccupation

"Finally, brothers, whatever is true, whatever is noble, whatever is right, whatever is pure, whatever is lovely, whatever is admirable if anything is excellent or praiseworthy — think about such things."

— *Philippians 4:8*

When we are preoccupied with something, it means we allow our thoughts to focus on that thing for a significant amount of time. A growing preoccupation means that our obsession gradually increases as time passes, becoming harder to break and taking more of our energy and time away from other activities. Early in our addiction, we were "recreational users," limiting our acting out to our free time. As our addiction progressed, it began to intrude upon us at inappropriate times, like when we were supposed to be working, or paying attention at school, or while we were at church. We found ourselves loosing our ability to not think about our fantasies.

For example, Bob found that his occasional visits to a local strip club, on his way home from work, became more frequent over time. He started spending more time looking forward to the end of the workday, known as "watching the clock." He progressed to indulging his fantasies about his visits to the club throughout the day. Soon, he was making excuses to leave work early. He even began to lie to his boss and coworkers to cover his early exits. As his addiction progressed, he began to take his lunch hour there. Bob was spending less and less time on his job, or with his family, and friends. His preoccupation with lust was taking more and more of his energy and time.

Another example of progressing behaviors is found in Sharon's story. She had always been diligent about deleting porn emails, but one day, she let her curiosity get the better of her. She clicked on a link and found herself transported to a world she'd never seen before. The images were powerful and disturbing at the same time. She couldn't help stop herself from looking at image after image. Before she knew it, she had spent half a day cruising different porn sites. Even though she felt ashamed, she also felt thrilled. She swore she'd never do it again. Yet, time after time she found herself drawn back by the lure of seeing things she'd never seen before. She also discovered that she spent more time when she was away from the computer thinking about either what she had seen, or planning how to budget more time to get back on the net. In a few months, she had moved from not thinking about porn at all, to having a hard time in thinking about anything else.

As Paul tells us in Philippians, we should be preoccupied with Godliness. That way we become more Christ-like. We become the thing that we focus on: If we focus on porn we become more like the porn we view, but if we focus on Jesus, we bcome more like the Christ we see. If we measured the quantity of time you focus on Christ versus the amount of time you focus on lust, which is the greater portion? Which are you more like, Christ or lust?

Answer the following questions to help you define the development of powerlessness (dependence) in your own life.

1. Describe how your mind become more and more consumed by sexual thoughts and behaviors: _____

_____

_____

_____

_____

_____

2. Did you spend progressively less energy on non-sexual thoughts and behaviors? If yes, give an example of how. _____

_____

_____

_____

_____

_____

_____

3. How did your thoughts about sex change over time? _____

_____

_____

_____

_____

_____

_____

4. How did your perceptions of women (or other objects of your lust) change over time.

_____

_____

_____

_____

_____

5. Estimate how often you had sexual thoughts at the beginning of your addiction, and at the current time. Is there a progression? Or, are you like many alcoholics who, from the

first drink, drink until they black out? _____

6. Did the content of your sexual thoughts change with time? _____

7. Have you found yourself turning to sexual thoughts during times of stress? _____

8. When you are bored or alone, do you find yourself obsessing on sexual thoughts? ___

9. How did your sexual thoughts help you cope with your life, feelings and experiences?

10. Did your sexual thoughts get in the way of other activities (such as employment, family time, academics, hobbies, sports, or social activities)? If yes, describe how. _____

We've just taken a close look at how your addiction impacted your mind, in the form of a growing preoccupation. Now, let's look at how the addiction affected your behaviors.

Tolerance

> *"Man does not live on bread alone,*
> *but on every word that comes from the mouth of God."*
>
> *— Deuteronomy 8:3*

Many of us share the experience of getting bored with a certain behavior. We found that the things that used to be wonderfully exciting, ceased to be as effective after a while. We needed to "cross boundaries" to get the same high. Therefore, we graduated from softcore porn, to hardcore porn, or we moved beyond monogamous sex, to sex with multiple partners. The medical community describes this as "tolerance" or, needing more frequent or more intense experiences to achieve the same effect.

For example, why did Bob increase the number of times he visited the strip club? Why did he wind up staying longer with each visit? Because he "needed" more to achieve the same effect that the first visit had given him. At the first visit to a strip club, all the sights, sounds, and smells are new, exciting, and illicit. By the third or fourth visit to the club, the newness has worn off, and even the dancers are no longer as titillating as they were before. Bob found he had to stay longer, waiting for the "better" dancers to perform, and had to visit more often, hoping for new girls. Before long, that club was no longer exciting enough, and he began to cruise other clubs in town, driving farther and farther in search of that elusive high he had found in his first visit. Initially in Sharon's case, she had only been curious about heterosexual images, but she later began looking at lesbian, gay, and fetish images as well. The heterosexual images were no longer sufficient to interest her. In both cases, Bob and Sharon had developed a "tolerance" to experiences that had once been sufficient to excite them.

When we came to recovery, we found ourselves at a place where we realized that we "needed" our relationship with lust, and that it was destroying us. It was as if the need for lust was as critical as our need to breathe, to eat, or to sleep. In recovery, we learned that sex is not a need. We had confused our need for love, with our desire (or want) for sex, via the mixer of lust. We needed to discover that sex is entirely optional.

Crossing forbidden boundaries is common for addicts. When we engage in illicit behaviors, when we do things we are not supposed to do, it increases the high we get. The boundaries we cross could be emotional, psychological, sexual, or moral. However, we discovered a painful consequence of our boundary-busting behaviors was that when we violate someone else's boundaries, we also violate our own.

To understand the fullness of the depths of depravity that lust has caused us to sink to, we need to examine the boundaries that we crossed in pursuit of our sexual high. For example, staying up late to watch adult movies, or skipping meals to engage in sexual activities, are both examples of violating our own physical boundaries. Indulging sexual thoughts and behaviors frequently represents violations of our moral or religious boundaries. Peeping on a family member represents a violation of family boundaries, and a violation of someone else's personal boundaries. List the boundaries you crossed in order to get that "high" one more time.

Broken Boundaries

1. _____
2. _____
3. _____
4. _____
5. _____
6. _____
7. _____
8. _____
9. _____
10. _____
11. _____
12. _____
13. _____
14. _____
15. _____

Many of us found that it was also helpful to detail the progression of our tolerance, by detailing the progression of our behaviors from least explicit to most explicit. For example, if you started your sexual acting out career by masturbating to the underwear section of a Sears catalog, did you later move on to National Geographic, and then to Playboy magazine? Later still, did you move on to magazines that are more explicit or to actual physical contact with another person? Write out the progression of your lust from less explicit, to more explicit.

Progressing Behaviors

Less Explicit

Sears catalog _____

_____
_____
_____
_____
_____
_____

More explicit

National Geographic _____

_____
_____
_____
_____
_____
_____

Most Explicit

Playboy _____

_____
_____
_____
_____
_____
_____

Loss of Control

> *"All power wherever found is power for evil as well as for good; and the greater the power the greater the evil."*
>
> — Vincent McNabb

Powerlessness is also about loss of control. We found we were unable to control our lust. Like the alcoholic for whom the first drink inevitably leads to another and another, as sex addicts we cannot lust like normal people. Whatever "normal" lust is, ours goes way beyond that, and does not stop until it has destroyed us.

We learned we had lost control when we continued to indulge our lust, even after we promised ourselves and others that we would not. In our sincerest moments, erroneously believing it to be physically and mentally possible, we swore we would stop. However, as time passed, we forgot why we should not, we broke our promise to ourselves, and the insanity of our rationalizations brought us back to our lust, time and time again. Each time we wondered how it had happened, again.

We also learned that we had no control over our lust when we engaged in behaviors that violated our moral values. For example, we promised ourselves that we would only look at porn, but never engage in actual sex with another person, only to later find ourselves in a "morning after" scene. Or, perhaps we allowed ourselves to rationalize allowing our lust to impact our workplace – which we also swore we'd never do. And yet in spite of recognizing that these violations of our moral values were a red flag frantically waving, "Hey, you've got a problem here!" We marshaled on, telling ourselves, "next time" we won't do that…Right. Some people refer to this stage of the disease as when the tail began to "wag the dog."

A good example of loss of control is found in Sharon's story. She shared how she had initially begun looking at porn on the internet out of curiosity. Her lust quickly escalated to more "prohibited" images and eventually even the prohibited images were insufficient to satisfy her lust. She found herself crossing the boundaries in her real life and began to indulge fantasies about people she knew. Initially she engaged in some "harmless" flirtatious behaviors that she found thrilling. Sharon would build up a sexual excitement during the day and then act out with the internet at night. Nightime porn and chatrooms led to daytime flirtations. Many have said that if you can imagine yourself doing something you create a reality that you will eventually fulfill. Sharon did just that. Her nighttime fantasies began to revolve around a coworker with whom she wound up having an affair. What once would have been unthinkable to her – having an affair, and with a married man – had become her reality. After the first time, she swore to herself to never mix romance and workplace relationships again. However, her pain was soon forgotten and she returned to her nighttime fantasies and her daytime flirtations. Another affair followed, and she lost her job after that one. Looking back, Sharon describes this as the point where the "tail began to wag the dog".

Another example is our friend, Bob. In the last section, we saw how Bob was stealing time from his employer, and his family to go to the strip clubs. Eventually, his absenteeism and his poor work performance caught up to him. Bob's supervisor called him into his office and confronted him about these problems. Recognizing that he was in danger of losing his job, Bob looked with "new eyes" at his behavior. He agreed with his supervisor that his performance had slipped and assured the boss it would not happen again. He offered some vague excuse about being a little "burned out" and not being able to hold his "focus" very well. Bob honestly meant everything he said to his supervisor. As he returned to his own office his mind raced over his recent behaviors, and was overwhelmed by how much time he had lost in the strip clubs. "How could I have been so stupid?!" he thought. The clubs were definitely not worth losing his job over. He promised himself that he would stop.

Bob did stop for a while. Then, one afternoon, after a particularly stressful day, he passed by the strip club on his way home. "I'm really too stressed to drive," he said to himself. "I should stop in for a drink and relax a bit before I go home." He reasoned, "After all, I've earned some peace and quiet after today. I'll just stay for a little while." And Bob did stay for just a little while. The next week he stayed for just a little while longer. A few days later, he stopped in for lunch. Before long, he was back to his old pattern. Bob was out of control.

Use the following questions to examine the loss of control of sexual behaviors in your own life.

1. Were there times when you said you were going to stop the sexual behaviors and then you did not? Describe the experiments you tried to help you stop (e.g., promising yourself, God, or someone else; or limiting the behaviors or situations.) _____

_____
_____
_____
_____
_____

2. Did you violate personal or family morals, or religious values? If so, describe how and when. _____

_____
_____
_____
_____
_____

3. Did your compulsiveness cause you to change your attitude, behaviors, or feelings towards family members or others (e.g., breaking promises or appointments)? Write at least one example for each area where you changed. _____

_____
_____

_____
_____
_____
_____

4. In what areas of your life has your compulsiveness cost you something (e.g., a relationship, job, loss of money)? Write several examples. _____
_____
_____
_____
_____
_____
_____

5. Has your compulsive behavior cost you time away from friends, family, hobbies, your job, or church? If minutes were dollars, how much has your addiction cost you? _____
_____
_____
_____
_____
_____

6. Have you paid a cost with your physical health, either directly or indirectly? Direct consequences would be through a sexually transmitted disease, such as herpes, crabs, yeast infections, etc.... Indirectly would be through secondary consequences, such as loss of sleep from staying up late, which costs you your alertness at work the next day, or weight gain from not exercising so you can spend more time acting out. _____
_____
_____
_____
_____
_____

7. What effect has your indulgence to your sexual thoughts or behaviors had on your spiritual life? _____

_____
_____
_____
_____
_____

8. What rationalizations (reasons) have you used to enable you to continue engaging in these behaviors? Have you said to yourself, as Bob did, "I deserve it," or, "I can do it just this once," or, "I'll only stay for a little while?" _____

_____
_____
_____
_____
_____

9. What has your behavior cost your family? How have you injured them through your actions? _____

_____
_____
_____
_____
_____

Now that you've answered each of the above questions, re-read your answers again. Think about all that you have given up for your addiction. Has it been worth it? What do you have left? Do you see that you are not in control of your own behaviors as you thought you were? Is that a cost you are willing to continue to pay? Some people have said that addicts only become willing to give up their addictive behaviors when the pain of acting out becomes greater than the pain of not acting out. Everyone has different thresholds of pain.

At the time that Bob first came to program, his life was mostly destroyed. He was eventually fired from his job due to his excessive absences and poor performance. When he chose to tell his wife some of the truth about why he lost his job, she asked him to move out of the house. She felt betrayed sexually, interpersonally, and financially. She could no longer trust him to provide for and protect her and their children. If he wanted to have any chance for reconciliation, she required that he get some help for himself.

Reluctantly, Bob scheduled an appointment with a counselor recommended by his church. "I've had a string of bad choices and even worse luck," Bob told the counselor. "I realize how stupid I've been and don't want to lose my family," he said.

Dr. Jamison asked Bob whether there was a difference between "being stupid" and "having a problem" with sex. Bob thought that there was a really big difference and said so, "I'm not one of those guys who has affairs on his wife or something, I was just bored at work and made some bad choices out of that boredom. I needed a new job anyway."

"So you don't see going to strip bars as the same thing as having an affair?" asked Dr. Jamison.

Bob replied, "Well, it's not like I think it's a Godly thing to do, but it is certainly not like an affair...I mean I never had any feelings for the girls in the clubs, we never had a relationship."

"I see," said Dr. Jamison. "You know, Jesus said that if you look at a woman and lust after her that you have already committed adultery with her in your heart. So in Jesus' eyes, going to a strip club is the same thing as an affair." (Matthew 5:28)

"Really..." said Bob. "I guess I never thought of it that way before."

Bob had just experienced a small moment of spiritual awakening. In this case, he came to believe that one of his behaviors that he had rationalized as being not too bad, since it wasn't as bad as some other behaviors, was actually equally as bad as one of the worst behaviors he could imagine. As his mind opened itself to the reality of his moral failing, he began to see the truth of his problem in a new way: He realized that he had not been in as much control as he thought he had been.

In our next section, we will take a different approach to your addiction. In the following exercise you will take a "bird's eye view" of your addiction so that you can see the "big picture" that is your sexual life.

Sexual Behavior History

In this section you are going to document your history of sexual behaviors. Make a list of every sexual behavior and experience that you can remember. Begin with the earliest memory you have of sexual feelings or experiences. Be brief, but write enough about these events so that later you can re-read it, and remember what you are referring to. Be aware that you may have to revise or update this list as you remember more and more of your childhood. This may seem a bit overwhelming; so give yourself permission to spend plenty of time working this part of your first step. However, remember the principle of balance to life from "The Solution" ("each day...work some, play a little, sleep some, spend some time with a friend..."). Your first step does not have to be finished in one day.

When you have finished your list, you are ready to go on to the following section, the "Addiction History Timeline." In this section you will use your list to explore your addiction in greater depth. You could characterize this as moving from the "big picture" to the magnifying glass.

Addiction History Timeline

The Addiction History Timeline helps us to understand the impact our sexual experiences had upon us - how the experience changed us and is connected to the events that followed it. Sexual contact touches our self-esteem and feelings in a powerful way, especially when we are children.

The next page shows a five-column tool that we use to chronicle the development of our addiction over time. The five columns are: Age, Sexual Events, Feelings, Self-Statements, and Family Events. Each event that you chronicled in your sexual behavior history list is transferred to the "Sexual Events" column. You then detail your age when it happened, your feelings, impact on your self-esteem and any related family events. Examples for each are provided in the pages following the Timeline form. It might be a good idea to make a few copies of the worksheet before you start writing so that you will have plenty of space for your history. Alternately, some people just make their own table on their computer or notepads.

Sexual Events	Feelings	Self-Statements	Family Events

Age						

In the first two columns fill in the Sexual Events from your Sexual Behavior History list and your age at the time the event happened.

AGE	SEXUAL EVENT
5	Noticed that sister doesn't have one.
6	Older neighborhood boy showed me his father's PLAYBOY magazines.
6 1/2	Playing "doctor" with neighbor girl, getting caught by her mom.

In the third column, you document the feelings you experienced at the time of the event. For many of us this can be a difficult and challenging task. Our feelings were complicated and confusing, and many of us simply don't know what to call them. For most of us, early sexual experiences created many different types of feelings. For example, we may have felt curiosity, shock, numbness, embarrassment, pain, anger, hurt, discomfort, confusion, fear, anxiety, excitement, rage, lust, or shame. Many of these feelings may have happened all at once and may be difficult to sort out these many years later. Therefore, many of us found it helpful to talk to a trusted person to help us sort out all of these emotions.

Addiction History Timeline: Feelings

AGE	SEXUAL EVENT	FEELINGS
5	Noticed that sister doesn't have one.	Puzzlement, anxiety.
6	Older neighborhood boy showed me his father's PLAYBOY magazines.	Curiosity, excitement, fear & anxiety.
6 1/2	Playing "doctor" with neighbor girl, getting caught by her mom	Excitement, lust, & shame.

As difficult as sorting out our emotions was, the next step, identifying the negative self-statements that we developed as a result of these experiences, was even more so. As the shame increases in frequency and intensity, our feelings because of the event become attached to our self-concept. For example, when you get caught acting out for the first time you are aware of certain bodily sensations such as a "hot face," or turning red from embarrassment, rapid and shallow breathing, or tears mixed with anger. Collectively these experiences feel "bad." The most common label for this experience is "shame." However, when shame attaches to the self we describe that as "toxic shame." What happened for many of us was that I "feel" bad became I "am" bad.

Addiction History Timeline: Self-Statements

AGE	SEXUAL EVENT	FEELINGS	SELF-STATEMENTS
5	Noticed that sister doesn't have one.	Puzzlement, anxiety.	"I am different."
6	Older neighborhood boy showed me his father's PLAYBOY magazines.	Curiosity, excitement, fear & anxiety.	"I am behaving badly."
6 1/2	Playing "doctor" with neighbor girl, getting caught by her mom	Excitement, lust, & toxic shame.	"I am bad."

Recovery has shown us that all of our early experiences happened in the context of our family, and our family's circumstances at that time. Everything that happens affects everything else. Consider the glassy-smooth surface of a pond early in the morning. A small stone dropped into the center will create small, ever-widening ripples, which soon stretch to touch every square inch of shoreline. The same thing happens with the smallest of "stones" that are dropped into the middle of our lives. Consider then, how powerful the impact of the larger "boulders" had upon our lives.

Document in the "Family Events" column, the stones and boulders which were dropped into the middle of your life. Examples of these events include: divorce of parents, the coming or going of significant others in your life, deaths, marriages, births, moving, graduating, vacations, holidays, new jobs, losing jobs, beginning or ending of a dating relationship (yours, a parents', or other family member), abusive experiences (physical, sexual, or emotions: yours or a significant others'), wars, natural disasters, and your or other family member's physical or emotional illness. Many of these events are connected to acting out events. Some of them were not, but we still examine the negative self-statements that came out of the Family Events.

Addiction History Timeline: Family History (Events)

AGE	MEMORY	FEELINGS	SELF-STATEMENTS	FAMILY EVENTS
5	Noticed that sister doesn't have one.	Puzzlement, anxiety.	"I am different."	Family moved.
6	Older neighborhood boy showed me his father's PLAYBOY magazines.	Curiosity, excitement, fear & anxiety.	"I am behaving badly."	Dad working 6 days/week, 12 hr./day.

| 6 1/2 | Playing "doctor" with neighbor girl, getting caught by her mom | Excitement, lust, & toxic shame. | "I am bad." | Parents divorced, dad moved out. |

Now that you have completed your timeline, take a mental step back to get a "bird's eye view" of your history. Do you find a correlation between the growing dependence, and the growing chaos in your family, or life? Does it occur to you that what has happened to you is bigger than you? Our narcissism would have us believe that everything happens either for us, or because of us. A more objective view shows us that we are just a small gear in a much, much larger machine. If it is true that our "problem" is larger than we are, then logically, our hope for recovery has to come from something larger than ourselves. How could we ever believe we could make it on our own?

Addiction History: Genogram

Let's take one more step back for an even larger view of the "big picture." It is an accepted fact that most addicts come from other addicts, genetically speaking. The majority of us inherited our addiction(s) from a parent or a grandparent. During this exercise, you will construct your genogram, or "family tree." A genogram is a graphical representation of your family that allows you to see patterns of behaviors and events that occurred in your family's history. In order to complete this exercise you may need to interview several members of your family to fill in the "blanks" where your own knowledge falls short.

The following types of information are of particular interest to you: marriages, divorces, extra-marital relationships, alcohol or chemical dependency, gambling, sex addiction, eating disorders, or compulsive spending. Additional information to note is the gender and number of children for each couple, physical illnesses, mental illness, births and deaths and dates for all of the above. Be willing to take risks to get this information, as this is an important part of your recovery.

You may have amends to make before you can complete this step. For example, you might need to call Aunt Ruth, whom you told off once, and have not spoken to in 15 years. Or you might have to take the risk of breaking the family's "rule of silence" that says, "We don't talk about those things. It's best not to drag up the past."

Some addictions, like alcoholism or drug addiction, are sometimes easy to spot. The path behind alcoholics and drug addicts are often littered with problems with the law, broken relationships and failed jobs. For the sex addict, many of our behaviors are secretive and not generally known. However, we have found that if we ask specific questions of a willing witness, we can sort the truth out. When individuals are uncomfortable with the topic, we respect their boundaries and do not press.

Genogram Symbols

The following key explains the symbols used in building a genogram.

○ = Female   □ = Male

○─┬─□ Two people connected by a relationship. In this case, they are married, and
m. 1978   the date of marriage is noted underneath.

□─//─○ The broken line symbolizes a divorce and the dates of marriage and
m. 1984   divorce are noted underneath.
d. 1988

⊠ A gender symbol with an "X" through it symbolizes a death, and the date
1993   and cause of death are noted underneath.
auto accident

TIP: Draw your genogram in black ink and use colored markers to note significant events or issues. Each issue should have its own color. For example, use red to denote alcoholism, green to denote mental illness, etc...

Start with yourself, your spouse and children, if you have them, near the bottom of the page, centered. Leave room beneath you for any grandchildren and their relatives you may have. Work your way out and up with your, and if you have one, your partner's family history.

A sample genogram is provided below. We have left off names to keep the graph simple for illustration purposes, and due to printing constraints, could not use color. Colors make it easier to see the patterns within a given generation and across several generations. What patterns do you see in your own genogram? Remember, since addictions tend to be inherited, chances are you got yours from someone you love!

Sample Genogram

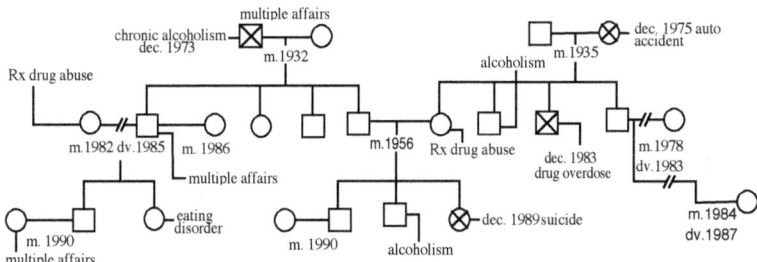

Once you have completed your own genogram, share it with someone who cares about you. Talk them through your family tree and help them see how the different addictions and problems have been passed from one generation to the next. Don't be surprised if you find that a particular addiction "skips" a generation. The children of an alcoholic might be "tea-totalers" but their own children could still be alcoholics. Does your genogram help you see how your addiction is much bigger than you are? If it was able to ensnare generations of your own family, do you really stand any kind of a chance against it on your own?

Now, take out a piece of paper and write a summary paragraph or two about your addiction. State as clearly as you are able, what you have learned about your own powerlessness. Before you start, read your First Step one more time. Many of us found it helpful to wait a few days or a week to re-read our First Step before we wrote these paragraphs.

Congratulations! You have now completed your first, First Step. Be sure to share it with someone who cares about you, such as a sponsor or your home group.

Step Two

Came to believe that God could restore us to sanity.

> "There cannot be a God because if there were one,
> I could not believe that I was not He."
>
> — *Friedrich Nietzsche*

Late one afternoon, Sharon's boss stopped by her desk and asked her to come to her office. "Uh-oh," Sharon thought to herself. "I'm in trouble."

Her boss got right to the point, "Sharon, we hired you knowing that your recommendations were not good. We decided to take a chance on you. But you let this company down. You can't expect to keep a job when you don't get your work done and when your lunches go two hours when you are scheduled for 45 minutes. We've given you numerous warnings and reprimands and you have not made the requisite changes in behavior. I'm sorry, but we're going to have to let you go, effective immediately."

The woman paused for a moment, letting the news sink in, and then she gently said, "Sharon, you were an exemplary employee for your first two months here. However, these past three months have been…well…unacceptable. What happened?"

Sharon had been staring at the table, unable to meet the woman's eyes. Slowly she looked up to meet her gaze. "I…ah, got involved with someone."

"I see," said her boss. "Off the record Sharon?" she asked.

"Sure, ok." said Sharon.

"I'm telling you this because I like you, and off the record because I can't be getting into the personal life of an employee, but I guess since you're officially fired, you're not an employee anymore." She paused a moment, "Anyway, your last boss told me that this was a pattern with you – that when you got involved with someone you neglect your work and had lost previous jobs for the same reason. I didn't believe him. I thought maybe you'd gotten a raw deal because the person was an executive in the company." Sharon just stared at table, unable to think of anything to say. "I don't want to know if the person you are currently involved with is an employee here or not, Sharon. But I think you need to take a serious and hard look at how you allow your personal relationships to interfere with your work performance."

The meeting ended soon after and Sharon was escorted by company security to clean out her desk, asked for her key card and parking placard, and then escorted to the front door. As she placed her personal belongings into her car, climbed in and closed the door she thought to herself, "Great. You've really done it this time, Sharon. Once again, you can't keep your bedroom out of the boardroom. NOW what are you going to do?!"

When we first realized that we were "powerless" over lust and that our lives had become unmanageable, we were overwhelmed by our hopelessness. We realized that we were lost without a power greater than our selves. When we walked into this program, others told us that there was hope for our recovery through the grace and love of Jesus.

Did we dare to hope in the concept of a God out there, who, being more powerful than we are, was strong enough to restore our sanity? There had to be, or else there would be no hope.

For many of us, working the Second Step stirred up many difficult feelings. Some of us have sworn off believing in a God who would let us suffer the way we have, one who would not answer our desperate prayers. Others have been offended by the apparent hypocrisy of religious leaders. Still others have never believed in all that supernatural hocus-pocus. For whatever reason, discussions about faith are always sure to bring up something passionate in each of us. Because of that, be aware that you might need support while you work this step, and you could require more resources than this guide provides. We have included a bibliography at the end referring you to additional resources that have been helpful to us. Additionally, we recommend that you take the step to reach out to a pastor in your area, or other spiritual mentor whom you respect, to assist you in resolving any issues of theology or spirituality.

Came to believe...

The phrase, "Came to believe..." implies an emerging process, more than a sudden revelation, or insight. It is the past tense of the verb, "come," which means, "to travel toward." In the Alcoholics Anonymous verbal tradition, this step involves three separate phases: first, "we came"; second, "we came to"; and third, "we came to believe." In the first stage, we came to these rooms, confused and bewildered, angry and resentful, distraught and hopeless, or just brought our bodies, while our minds were elsewhere. In the second stage, we "came to" – as in waking up. Most of us had been walking around in the fog of our addictions for a long time. The longer we stayed abstinent from our addictions, the clearer our mind became. Ultimately, we came "to believe" in the possibility that there could be a God who might be able to restore us to sanity. As you work this step, keep in mind that your spiritual growth will continue long after you have moved on in your working of the other steps in this program.

Sharon went where many people go when they don't know where else to turn; she went to church. Well, actually, she went to the internet and conducted a search for resources for people with "relationship problems." Imagine her surprise to find herself directed to the website of a large, local church with a "recovery program." At her first meeting, she felt awkward and obvious, but several of the other women seemed to go out of their way to greet her and help her to feel welcome. As she listened to others share their stories, Sharon realized that her own story was not really so unique. She saw something in these women that she did not have in her own life - hope. She wondered whether there was any hope for her.

Sharon had grown up in a Christian home, and went to church and Sunday school every week until she went off to college. However, she was never certain if God was real, or just the product of people who need a "crutch" to get through life. However, when she was not able to pay her rent for the second month in a row because she could not get another job due to her poor references, she remembered the God of her youth and prayed, "God, if you are real, I need your help. I don't know where to turn, or how I will pay my bills. Please help me." Her family had disowned her, and her friends were all too busy with their own lives to attend to the most recent crisis in a long, long string of crises in her life. Sharon felt lost and completely alone for the first time in her life. She had reached her "bottom."

In the darkness of her room that night, Sharon waited for a sign of some type from God: A light from heaven, or an angelic choir, but there was nothing except the quiet sound of her own breathing. She mumbled, "Figures," and rolled over to go to sleep. In the morning, she barely noticed that she had slept soundly for the first time in many months.

Eventually, Sharon found another job, and after many months of scrimping and saving, she was able to get caught up on her rent. It wasn't until she began to think about what she was going to share at her next meeting that she realized how much her life had changed since she first came to program. She remembered that night so many months previously when she had prayed to God for help and waited vainly for a sign from Him. She realized that He had actually answered her prayers after all. "Perhaps it is possible," Sharon said to her group, "that God really does exist!"

Many of us have shared the same awakening of spirituality as Sharon's story illustrates.

...that God...

When we were lost in the insanity of our addiction, we found that our perceptions about God became tainted by the pain and suffering we had endured. We prayed to God and asked Him to remove our compulsion to act out only to wind up doing the same things again, and again. This caused our perception of God to change into a distant, uncaring God who claimed He had the power to raise the dead, and yet who refused to answer even our simplest prayers.

Psalm 142

To God I made my sorrows known,
From God I sought relief;
In long complaints before his throne
I poured out all my grief.

My soul was overwhelmed with woes,
My heart began to break;
My God, who all my burden knows,
He knows the way I take.

On every side I cast mine eye,
And found my helpers gone;
While friends and strangers passed me by,
Neglected or unknown.

Then did I raise a louder cry,
And called thy mercy near,
Thou art my portion when I die;
Be thou my refuge here.

Lord, I am brought exceeding low,
Now let thine ear attend,
And make my foes who vex me know
I've an almighty Friend.

From my sad prison set me free,
Then shall I praise thy name,
And holy men shall join with me
Thy kindness to proclaim.

— *The Psalms and Hymns of Isaac Watts*

What god would promise to answer our prayers, yet not grant this one simple request: "Help me stop!" Were we not "good enough" Christians? Perhaps we didn't pray hard enough? Sometimes we wondered if God was punishing us because of our sin, or worse, that maybe God didn't care enough about us to answer our prayers?

So where, you ask, is hope? In program, hope arrives in two forms: 1) we had to learn that we are not alone in our struggle, and 2) we had to learn that God is not to blame for our lack of sobriety.

It is good to know that we are not alone in our struggle. It helps us to feel a little less defective, doesn't it? Or, perhaps you might be thinking, "Great, now instead of being the only rotten apple, I'm in a barrel chock-full of rotten apples!" Well, either way you choose to look at it, learning that God does not have a personal vendetta against us allows us to let go of some of our anger at Him.

Working our program helped us to learn several essential truths about ourselves, and about God. First, we had to learn that He is God, and we are not. Secondly, we learned there a few things that God cannot do. One thing that God cannot do is to violate our free will. If we give our lust to Him, and then take it back, He will not stop us. The bottom line is that if we can't keep our sobriety, it is not because He has failed us, it is because we have failed ourselves. Another thing we learned about God is that He is always faithful and constant.

Step Two has often been referred to as "The Hope Step." With this step, there is hope for recovery; without it, all is lost. We have learned that we cannot start where we are not, we have to start where we are. Therefore, if you have no hope right now, then start with hoping for hope. Only when we surrender ourselves can we truly allow God to work in our lives.

Does God Exist?

"I have read in Plato and Cicero sayings that are very wise and very beautiful; but I never read in either of them: 'Come unto me all ye that labour and are heavy laden.'"

— *St. Augustine*

Martin Luther struggled with understanding the concept of how a loving God could condemn sinners. How could He condemn His own creation for a defect that He created? After all, He made us this way, right? Luther says he "meditated night and day" until he finally understood that God, himself, provided the solution. When we allow God to live in us, He infuses us with His own essence and power. That is how the unjust become justified. That is how the unrighteous become righteous. It is not in and of ourselves, but by God living in us. That is why we can have hope. By drawing first upon the strength we find in one another, we find that together we can begin to stay sober long enough to allow God to make us even stronger yet. Praise God. For it is by His stripes that we are healed. Amen!

Are you ready to begin the journey to hope? Let's start with defining what you currently believe about God. Who is God?

_____
_____
_____
_____

Write down as many adjectives as you can think of to describe God. _____
_____
_____
_____
_____
_____

We can know there is a divine, Creator God in one of two ways: General Revelation or Special Revelation. "General Revelation" is God's way of revealing Himself to us through nature and observable phenomenon. For example, more astronomers have concluded that there is a creator God since the advent of the Hubble telescope than before. Why is this true? Because with the Hubble telescope they have been able to peer into the deep reaches of the Universe and have not only found no evidence of life anywhere else in the Universe, but have also concluded that the third rock from our sun is the ONLY place in the Universe where life could exist!

General Revelation

"The heavens declare the glory of God; the skies proclaim the work of his hands."

— Psalm 19:1

Many of you have heard the "watchmaker" analogy, proving the existence of God. For those of you who have not, we offer it here. Imagine you find a watch and that you have never seen a watch and have no clue as to its function. However, the complexity of its design implies the existence of a watchmaker who designed and crafted it. If you apply that same logic to observable phenomenon about our world, it is clear that there was an "intelligent" designer to the earth and the entire universe. What do you think; is there a God? Here are a few facts from general revelation (please note this is not an exhaustive list) for you to consider. Did you know?:
- If the earth was 10% larger, or smaller, life would not exist on earth.
- If the earth was closer or farther away from the sun, life on earth could not exist.
- If the tilt of the earth's axis (23%) were not just so, then great masses of ice would form at the poles and the middle would be intolerably hot; again life would not exist.
- Every day, hundreds of thousands bolts of lightning strike the earth, bringing thou-

sands of tons of nitrogen into the soil, without which the plants would die.
- Water, which exists nowhere else in the universe in such abundance as on earth, expands when frozen and contracts when heated, the opposite of everything else. Also, it is lighter when frozen and without this property, all the rivers and lakes would freeze from the bottom up – killing all aquatic life during the winter.
- Evolutionary theory says that the fossil record shows the progression of life from simple organisms to more complex organisms – an "evolution" of form following a need. When drawn on paper evolutionary theory looks like a tree, with the start of life as the bottom of the trunk (no roots), and then the branches above becoming more diverse and complicated as life "branches" off into new creatures. In reality, the fossil record shows the exact opposite: that at one point in history, the Cambrian Period, there was a virtual "explosion" of life. Literally overnight, thousands of forms of life appear in the fossil record with no precursors, and then over time many of those life forms have died off. So the "evolutionary tree" as substantiated by the fossil record is actually an "upside down" tree, with the complex giving way to the more simple. Evolutionary theory is NOT supported by the fossil record. Even Darwin himself said that unless someone else could explain the problem of the Cambrian explosion that its existence made his theory untenable.

When learning about Chaos Theory – which says that **any** system tends towards disorder over time, moving from complex to simple – a fifth grader asked his science teacher that if that is true, how can evolutionary theory, which says that life progressed from simple to complex, hold true? The teacher responded, "That's a good question, let me get back to you on that." She emailed the question to a friend of hers, a high school science teacher, who responded simply, "That's why we have religion."

Do you believe there was an "intelligent designer" to life on earth? Even those of us who admit that there must be an intelligent designer, may still be reluctant to believe that such a being as a "personal" god. Perhaps you have had a negative experience with a religious organization, such as a Church? Many of us have. However, we have also found that organized religion is "not God" anymore than we are.

"The first time I saw Brother Lawrence was upon the 3rd of August, 1666. He told me that God had done him a singular favor, in his conversion at the age of eighteen. That in the winter, seeing a tree stripped of its leaves, and considering that within a little time, the leaves would be renewed, and after that the flowers and fruit appear, he received a high view of the Providence and Power of GOD, which has never since been effaced from his soul. That this view had perfectly set him loose from the world, and kindled in him such a love for GOD, that he could not tell whether it had increased in above forty years that he had lived since."

— *Brother Lawrence*

Think about the experiences you have had in your life when you thought, "Wow, there IS a God." When were the moments where you looked at something and knew with quiet certainty that the mountain, or that tree, or that baby was clear evidence of a creator-God? Now, write down three ways that you know that God exists from general revelation:

1) _____
2) _____
3) _____

Special Revelation

> *"I am the Alpha and the Omega," says the Lord God,*
> *"who is, and who was, and who is to come, the Almighty."*
>
> *— Revelations 1:8*

The second way we can know that God exists is by His "special revelation"– The Holy Bible. Many of us accept the Bible as God's perfect and inspired special letter to us. Many others of us have various issues with that notion. While it is beyond the scope of this step study to explore the fullness of that claim, we list a few sources in the reference list for you to examine. For those who struggle with the concepts of "inspired and perfect", we suggest you simply take the verses at face value and ask the Lord to help you with your uncertainty about the perfection of His Word.

Let's start by focusing on your knowledge of His Word. What are your favorite verses where God declares His existence? In what verses does God declare His characteristics? Write down three verses that you know. Here are a couple of example verses:

a) God is all-knowing: Psalms 33:13-15 From heaven the LORD looks down and sees all mankind; from his dwelling place he watches all who live on earth — he who forms the hearts of all, who considers everything they do.

b) God is spirit: John 4:24 God is spirit, and his worshipers must worship in spirit and in truth."

1) _____
2) _____
3) _____

Here are a few more verses about God that you may want to look up: Psalms 117:2, Matthew 19:26, Acts 26:8, Psalms 139:3, Acts 17:24, Matthew 6:26, 2 Corinthians 5:18, First Thessalonians. 5:9, James 4:12, Psalms 57:10, Romans 1:20, Ecclesiastes 3:11, Psalms 19:1.

Who is God to You?

> *"God is more truly imagined than expressed, and He exists more truly than He is imagined."*
>
> – Saint Augustine

Psychologists have determined that we get our perceptions of our Heavenly Father directly from our experience of our Earthly father. For many of us our Earthly fathers were, at best, far from perfect. In fact, research consistently shows that the majority of people (as high as 80%), who self-identify as sexual addicts, experienced some form of abuse in childhood. Some of that abuse happened at the hands of our fathers, or in our father's absence, or while he was too busy to notice. So some of us got a double-dose of Earthly-dad perceptions superimposed on our concept of our Heavenly father.

The first part of this assignment will require you to stop working this step, at least for a little while. Get your childhood photo album(s) and spend some time reviewing your history. For some of us, this step stirs up many feelings, so take your time and be willing to take good care of yourself. Call your sponsor and accountability partners so they can be praying for you, and be available if you need to talk. Some of you may not have any photos to review, so in that case, we'll use the guidance of the Holy Spirit and your memory. Find a quiet corner by yourself, and ask the Holy Spirit to guide you as you review your childhood memories. Ask Him to remind you of the memories you need to deal with, and to give you His wisdom to understand how all these pieces fit together. Come back when you've completed your walk down memory lane

Now that you've returned, take a few moments to write down as many adjectives as you can think of to describe your father (or primary male figure(s) from your childhood years).

_____
_____
_____
_____
_____

Flip back to your list of adjectives about God. When Sharon did this exercise she found that the adjectives she used for God were accurate, but lacked any real meaning to her. The more she thought about it the more she realized that she did not really KNOW God, certainly not in the same way she knew her father, grandfather, or one of her mom's brothers. Some of the words she had used were purely "head knowledge" – meaning that she knew those were God's characteristics because she learned it in Sunday school, but she did not know those characteristics at a personal level. When she re-evaluated her list, she threw all the words out that had no personal meaning. Now she had a significantly short list! Take a moment to do the same thing for yourself.

Now, compare the list of adjectives you wrote about God, to the list of adjectives you wrote about your father. Do you see any similarities? Well, those similarities are the bad news in that they have functioned as a ceiling on your experience of God. The good news is that God is not the same as your earthly father!

What type of earthly father did/do you have? Here are some adjectives commonly used: absent, abusive, distant, rejecting, loving, supportive, kind, anxious, angry, brooding, or teasing.

Write in the one word which best describes your dad, here: _____.
Now choose one word which best describes your perception of God: _____.
How similar are they and in what ways? _____
_____
_____
_____

Take a few minutes to write about the differences between your earthly and heavenly fathers. _____
_____
_____
_____
_____
_____
_____
_____
_____
_____
_____
_____

If you are like most of us, the lens of your earthly father has blurred your image of God. Starting today, make this your prayer, "Dear God, help me to see you with clear eyes, and to see you fully and truthfully."

...could restore us to sanity.

> *"When they came to Jesus, they saw the man who had been possessed by the legion of demons, sitting there, dressed and in his right mind; and they were afraid."*
>
> — *Mark 5:15*

In the Gospels, the authors tell us of an encounter between Jesus and a man who was possessed by so many demons that they went by the name Legion. (The word "legion" at that time was a military term that referred to a unit of 3,000 to 6,000 men in the Roman army.) This man appeared to be certifiably crazy. He lived alone in a desolate place and, night and day, he would smash himself with stones. The people of his town had tried to protect him from himself by chaining him, but he was so strong he would break the chains, and go right back to beating himself. With a few words, Jesus cast the demons out of him and restored his "right mind."

Many, if not all of us, have prayed that Jesus would restore our "right minds" with a lightning bolt, or whatever He uses for such miracles. Few of us, however, have had Jesus miraculously take away our addictive tendencies in the blink of an eye. Most of us, fortunately, can testify that God has transformed our lives by renewing our minds, one day at a time.

Ramone, for example, found that as soon as he stopped looking at porn on the internet, his craving to do so began to evaporate. Additionally, he noticed that the more he spent time with his wife and son, the more he realized that what porn was offering him was an illusion of intimacy, a lie in the truest sense of the word. He realized he was falling prey to the propaganda of the sex-trade business. They showed him an image of what sexuality "should" look like and then provided an easy (and the only) source of that sexuality via their offerings. Restored to his "right mind", Ramone realized that his wife is not a sexual slave, there to appease his slightest whim or desire, but rather a daughter of the most high God, entrusted to him by her Father, to be his partner in this life. Her sexuality is a product of her love for him, not to be used and taken for granted, but to be nurtured by him by cherishing her and their time together.

How much renewing of your mind will it take for you to be "restored to sanity"? How much power does Jesus have? Look up the following verses and describe what miracle Jesus performed.

Verse	Miracle
Matthew 8:1-4	_____
Mark 4:35-41	_____
Luke 5:17-26	_____

Matthew 9:27-31 _____

_____
_____
_____

Luke 7:11-17_____

_____
_____
_____

1) How does reading about these miracles impact you? Do you believe that Jesus actually performed them? Do you believe He can still perform them? _____

_____
_____
_____

How much power does Jesus have? He had enough power to cast out demons that could make a man so strong that he could not be bound by any other man nor confined by any chain made by man. He had enough power to cause the blind to see, the deaf to hear, the lame to walk, to cure leprosy, and to make the dead to live again (Luke 7:22). Is that enough power for you? We came to these rooms of recovery – definitely not in our right minds, and then we "came to" or began to see things more clearly, and finally we "came to believe" in a God who could restore our sanity. How big is God? Is He truly powerful enough to restore your right mind?

There is no question about God's ability or His willingness. The only questions have to do with OUR ability and OUR willingness to let Him. If we dare to truly surrender our right to indulge our own lustful thoughts, He will be faithful to restore our minds.

3) Is there anything that stands in your way to believing that God can restore your sanity? If yes, what is it?_____

_____
_____
_____
_____

4) If you do believe that God can restore your sanity, are you ready to allow Him to do so? If yes, tell someone else (accountability partner, sponsor, a friend) about your commitment and ask them to support you as you journey further down the road to recovery. Write the name(s) of the people you will invite to support you here: _____

_____
_____
_____
_____
_____

    For those who are having trouble connecting with God, we recommend a prayer that has helped many others connect with the Holy Spirit. It is the Prayer of St. Ambrose, of Milan. Find a quiet comfortable place where you feel safe. Take a few deep breaths to relax your body and mind, and then pray:

    "Oh Lord, teach me to seek you, and reveal yourself to me when I seek you. For I cannot seek you unless you first teach me, nor find you unless you first reveal yourself to me. Let me seek you in longing, and long for you in seeking. Let me find you in love, and love you in finding. Amen."

    Prayer is a private conversation between you and God. Whenever you set aside some bit of time to talk to God, we recommend you also read a few verses in the Bible. If you are unfamiliar with the Bible, we suggest you start with the Gospel of John. After that, you may want to read the book of Acts. Additional recommendations for Bible study resources can be found in the Bibliography.

Step Three

We made a decision to turn our wills and our lives over to the care of God.

> "No action will be considered blameless, unless the will was so, for by the will the act was dictated."
>
> — Seneca

Bob kept promising himself that he would leave after the next dancer. Yet when the next dancer left the stage, he didn't move. "Last one. For sure." Bob thought to himself. Eventually Bob did leave, after all of his tip money ran out. He tried to make up some of the time by speeding on the way home. He took out some of his frustrations by unleasing tirades on other drivers who were obnoxiously going the speed limit. Parking with care so as to not squeal the tires, he jumped out of his car, almost sprinted to the front door of what used to be his house, and rang the bell.

"You're late...again" accused his wife as she opened the door. Your son wouldn't let us light the candles on his cake until you got here. I can't believe you missed his entire birthday dinner! You're even more irresponsible now than you were before we separated!" Before he could say anything she turned her back on him and stormed out of his presence.

At the moment, Bob was having a hard time believing it himself. "Why didn't you just leave!?!" Bob thought angrily to himself. Mustering up as much positive energy as he could, he took a deep breath and went in to face his son and the rest of the family.

Every time we have struggled with lust, we made a choice: A small and quiet choice. We did not consciously make a choice to hurt someone we love, or a choice to do wrong simply for the sake of doing wrong, but rather a choice to indulge a thought. It was, after all, just a small and harmless thought. It felt so much better to let it run its course. The specifics of the thought vary from person to person, but the outcome is always the same: Lust.

We always knew it was wrong to indulge these thoughts, especially when we were young, we actually felt guilt and shame over their very existence in our heads. However, eventually the guilt and shame faded away in the face of the ecstasy. We quickly learned that the less we thought about what we wanted to do and just did it, the less we had to feel that awful guilt and shame, and the sooner we could get to the ecstasy. Over time, our conscience became seared, and we cared less and less about whether what we were doing was right or wrong.

In Step 1, we looked at our own powerlessness; that our lives had become unmanageable. In Step 2, we found our hope in God, that He has the power to return us to sanity. Step 3 is where we actually give the "reigns" of our lives over to His care. More than just requiring us to confess our faith in God, Step 3 challenges us to turn over our "right" to continue in our relationship with lust.

Dr. Jekyll and Mr. Hyde

> *"I was stepping leisurely across the court after breakfast, drinking the chill of the air with pleasure, when I was seized again with those indescribable sensations that heralded the change; and I had but the time to gain the shelter of my cabinet, before I was once again raging and freezing with the passions of Hyde. It took on this occasion a double dose to recall me to myself; and alas! six hours after, as I sat looking sadly in the fire, the pangs returned, and the drug had to be re-administered. In short, from that day forth it seemed only by a great effort as of gymnastics, and only under the immediate stimulation of the drug, that I was able to wear the countenance of Jekyll. At all hours of the day and night, I would be taken with the premonitory shudder; above all, if I slept, or even dozed for a moment in my chair, it was always as Hyde that I awakened. Under the strain of this continually impending doom and by the sleeplessness to which I now condemned myself, ay, even beyond what I had thought possible to man, I became, in my own person, a creature eaten up and emptied by fever, languidly weak both in body and mind, and solely occupied by one thought: the horror of my other self."*
>
> — *Robert Louis Stevenson*
> The Strange Case of Doctor Jekyl and Mr Hyde

    In program we often refer to "our addict" and we talk about "Dr. Jekyll and Mr. Hyde." In this case, Dr. Jekyll is the good person who interacts with the world, and Mr. Hyde, is our addict, who does what he wants, when he wants. Over time, we found that Mr. Hyde had taken on a life of his own. We were out of control, and could not stop. Our lives had become unmanageable.

    We did what we did mostly in secret. After all, since what we were doing was wrong, if we told someone, we would have to stop feeling good. Lusting was one of the few things in life that could make us feel good. So, by living part of our life in secret, and the rest of it pretending the other part did not exist, we created a split in our selves: A "good" self to show the world, and our "bad" and secret self.

    Others of us dropped all pretenses at hiding what we were doing. We had become calloused and dared anyone to challenge our right to do what we wanted. We rationalized our behaviors and challenged all societal institutions like monogamy and marriage as being archaic and unrealistic for today's forward thinking people. We considered all religion as being constructed by powerful people to control weaker people. So with no ultimate authority to curtail us, we kicked Dr. Jekyll to the curb.

Faith

"Faith is trust, and it is therefore primarily volitional and emotional. Belief, on the other hand, is primarily intellectual: it is the assent of the mind. But while belief is not itself faith, faith where there is no belief in something is quite impossible."

— *Edwin Lewis*

In sobriety, we have learned how to face our lives with new courage. We discovered that God was God and we were not. Our ability to wreck our own lives was outpaced only by our ability to wreck the lives of those around us. Therefore, we learned that we had to choose to trust God with our lives; that perhaps He would be better at running us than we were. Certainly, He would be hard pressed to make more of a mess than we already had. This step required of us a leap of faith: We would have to trust in the unknown and the untried.

So, what "God" do you believe in that you choose to turn the care of your life over to? There are many gods, but only one true God, with only one true Son and Savior. In Step 2, we examined your beliefs about the creator God. In Step 3 we need to examine your beliefs about a personal Savior: someone who not only cares enough about your life to be intimately involved on a daily basis with you, but who has the power to help change your life!

As humans, we were designed to need a relationship with God; therefore, there is a power in having a god, regardless of the power of the god. However if the god has no power to change your life, he's not much of a god, is he? Who is your personal savior?

Who is Jesus of Nazareth?

"I know men; and I tell you that Jesus Christ is no mere man. Between him and every other person in the world there is no possible term of comparison. Alexander, Caesar, Charlemagne, and I myself have founded empires; but upon what do these creations of our genius depend? Upon force. Jesus alone founded His empire upon love; and to this very day millions would die for him."

— *Napoleon Bonaparte*

Men have said that Jesus was a liar, a lunatic, or exactly who He said he was; the Son of God. Many say that Jesus was only a good teacher, like Buddah or Ghandi. The problem is, Jesus taught that He was the only begotten Son of God, and that He had the power to heal the sick, cause the blind to see, the lame to walk, to raise the dead back to life, and, oh yea, to forgive sins. You see, of all the "good teachers" in the world, none ever claimed to forgive sin. However, Jesus did. So if the things he said about himself were not true, he would be a very bad teacher, indeed, even a liar. Alternately, perhaps he was just a self-deluded lunatic. What do you think?

Jesus' Claims

> *"A man who can read the New Testament and not see that Christ claims to be more than a man, can look all over the sky at high noon on a cloudless day and not see the sun."*
>
> — William E. Biederwolf

Who did Jesus claim to be? Look up the following scriptures from the Book of John:

5:24 _____

6:35 _____

6:51 _____

10:9 _____

10:11 _____

11:25 _____

14:6 _____

If you have never taken the time to consider Jesus' claims about Himself, and are not certain, stop now and take the time to read the entire Book of John. Are you ready? Now, answer this question for yourself: "Who is Jesus of Nazareth?"

❏ A Liar   ❏ A Lunatic   ❏ The Son of God

If you have never asked Jesus to be your Lord and Savior, pray this prayer right now: "Dear Jesus, I admit that I am not perfect, that I have sinned, and that I need a Savior. I confess that you are the Son of God and ask you to forgive me of my sins and be my Lord and Savior. Amen."

If you have prayed that prayer before, now might be a good time to "rededicate" your life to Him. Take a moment to do so now.

If you have either prayed the "sinner's prayer" for the first time, or re-dedicated your life to Christ, you need to become part of a Christian community. You are now an "adopted" child of God, so take your place at the dinner table with the rest of the family! Welcome! We rejoice that you are here. Please start visiting some Churches in your area and find one where you feel the presence of God and where you feel comfortable with the people.

Restored to Sanity

So we believe there is a God, but do we believe that He can (or will) restore us to sanity? What does it mean to be restored to sanity? In its simplest form, it means to renovate the basic form and structure of what we believe. This may be the hardest part of this Step. In Romans, 12:2 Paul writes,

> "Do not conform any longer to the pattern of this world, but be transformed by the renewing of your mind. Then you will be able to test and approve what God's will is — his good, pleasing and perfect will."

It is this "renewing" of our minds that must take place for our sanity to be restored. Remember, this is a process that you begin today, more accurately; it is a skill that you need to learn. You see the problem is not what you think it is. On the other hand, the problem is exactly what you think.

Finding Bottom

> "Remorse: beholding heaven and feeling hell."
>
> — George Moore

To get to the place where we were willing to turn our lives over to the care of God, we had to face the reality of the wreckage we had inflicted on the world. The process of "finding bottom" is different for each of us, in the sense that some of us have to experience greater amounts of loss and pain than do others. However, for all of us, the process is, no more and no less than, whatever it takes to break through our denial that we have a problem.

Bob and Sharon both had to lose relationships and jobs before they were able to acknowledge that they had a problem with lust. Ramone, on the other hand, was caught by his son while he was looking at porn on the Internet. The loss of his son's respect for him was devastating and enough of a "wake up call" for Ramone to bring him to program. Whatever the nature and severity of the event(s) that God uses to break through our denial, they cause the scales to fall off our eyes so that we can see ourselves more clearly, in all of our depravity.

Dropping our distortions and rationalizations, we faced our sins and found the painful feelings called shame and remorse. Many people in program have told us that there is good news and bad news about getting into recovery: The good news is you get your feelings back; the bad news is you get your feelings back! The problem with shame and remorse is that they are lousy motivators. Humans tend to strongly dislike any contact with shame and remorse and go to great lengths to avoid it. What's the best way to stop feeling shame and remorse? Act out: But there you are, back where you started. In recovery, we had to learn new ways to deal with our shame and remorse. We started with being willing to go to whatever lengths were necessary to get and stay sober – in other words to not act out no matter what. That stopped the downward spiraling shame cycle. Then we had to learn a new way (vs acting out) to deal with our shame.

Here are some ways that we have learned to stop shaming ourselves and start healing ourselves: we challenged our "shoulds" and gave ourselves permission to be imperfect; we took risks by sharing openly about ourselves in meetings and were shocked when no one ran screaming from the room; we extended grace to others and found it easier to accept for ourselves; we prayed for God to help us see ourselves through His eyes – as fearfully and wonderfully made; and we prayed for courage to continue to work our program on a daily basis.

Write down three ways that you can practice receiving Grace today.

1) _____

_____

2) _____

_____

3) _____

_____

Surrender

"It is astonishing how the act of placing our own will as far as possible in unison with the Will of God restores our tranquility."

— Arthur Christopher Benson

What does it mean to "turn [your] life and will over to the care of God"? How, exactly, does one accomplish that feat? For many of us this simple task is easier to say than to do. We learned that to turn our lives over to God means to "surrender" our will to His. To surrender means to "abandon oneself entirely to." One way we learned to understand this concept was to give up our "right" to indulge lust and to act out. Since God cannot make us do something against our will, we have to continually give up our right to indulge what we want.

At first, we thought this was impossible. Our addict tried to convince us that we were unable to live without it, and in fact should not have to live without it! We tried to "white-knuckle" it, which is sort of like holding your breath; it only works for a very short while. However, every time we came back to our lust. Through trial and error, we eventually learned what it means to "abandon ourselves completely" to God's will.

Turning our lives over to God's care is not a feat of magic, but an act of the will. It is a choice, a decision to not indulge the thoughts that tempt us. Our addict can go from zero to sixty in zero point two seconds! It happens so fast we are not fully aware of the choices we have made that deliver us to the doorway of acting out. We just sort of find ourselves swept past the door and down the road to acting out before we know it. In recovery, we found that by not acting out we improved our ability to attend to the process of being tempted.

Write down three things that you need to do today to practice surrendering your will to God.

1) _____

_____

_____

2) _____

_____

_____

3) _____

_____

_____

Temptation

"When tempted, no one should say, "God is tempting me." For God cannot be tempted by evil, nor does he tempt anyone; but each one is tempted when, by his own evil desire, he is dragged away and enticed. Then, after desire has conceived, it gives birth to sin; and sin, when it is full-grown, gives birth to death."

— *James 1:13 - 15*

Have you ever thought much about how you come to do what you do? Not "why" – as in, "what were my motives," but *how* in a mechanical sense? What are the mechanisms in your mind that make it possible for a good person to do bad things?

What is James saying in the above verse? James asserts that you cannot be tempted by something that is not tempting to you. What is it that makes something tempting to you? It is your own evil desire. Next obvious question: "What is an 'evil desire'?" In it's simplest form, it is a belief. It is a belief that this thing – whatever it might be – is a "good" thing even though you know it to be wrong.

For example, Sharon believed it was wrong to have an intimate relationship with someone you were not married to, much less to do so with someone else's husband. How, then, did she wind up doing that which she did not believe in? For many of us, breaking these kinds of boundaries comes about from a series of subtle temptations, rather than the overt, "in your face" opportunities. In Sharon's case, she began by rationalizing her choice to look at sexual images of someone to whom she was not married.

Later, she began to indulge fantasies of people from her life and then to indulge in the "harmless" flirting. Flirtatious words eventually gave way to flirtatious touches – a touch on the shoulder here, a brush of the arm there. Lunches gave way to dinners. It wasn't so much that Sharon decided one day that she was going to have sex with a married man, she just continued to look the other way while she allowed this inevitability to mature.

An old analogy illustrates the principle effectively. Do you know how to boil a frog alive? (A disturbing image, but this is only an illustration, no actual frogs were harmed in the writing of this text.) If you drop a frog into a pot of boiling water, he will immediately jump right out. However, if you place the frog into a pot full of room temperature water, he will happily swim around. If you place the pot on the burner and turn up the heat, the frog will never notice the temperature change and will be boiled alive. This principle of "subtle temptation" is part of the mechanism that lets good people do bad things.

Satan's Lies

Cheap perfume and painted faces,
Fallen angels fill the places
Where I go, when my troubles pull me down.

All the lies I know they'll tell me
And the time that they will sell me
For a while, I'll be the biggest man in town.

— Randy Travis - "Promises"

Our evil desires are essentially beliefs that it would be "good" thing to do. We might define "good" as being exciting or fulfilling, or making us feel good in some way. For example, Bob realized that, while watching strippers perform created a pleasurable sensation in his head, it was the table dances that really became the source of temptation for him. Those dances created a pseudo-intimate moment, where the rest of the world disappeared, and it was only him and the dancer while the music played. Bob shared how he began to learn the schedules of his favorite dancers and to look forward to their performances, almost as if it was a date. "They're kind of like girlfriends to me, even though I know they're really not", he said. In this situation, Bob had developed a fantasy-belief that these girls actually cared about him.

We may be tempted because of real beliefs, or irrational fantasy beliefs. "Fantasy beliefs" are simply those belief structures which make sense in our fantasy worlds, but which don't hold up well under objective evaluation. Here are some other examples of the beliefs that we have found were part of our own evil desires:

a) the person (includes persons we encounter through photos, videos, phone, chat, or in-person) we are acting out with "really loves" us,

b) the other person is actually sexually attracted to us,

c) or that we are "special" to the other person in some way.

Not sure if you buy this notion that you actually believe, somewhere in your mind, that those things you've done which cause you shame are "good" ideas? In case you're having any trouble with that, think about it this way: If you didn't think there was something "good" about looking at pornography, you wouldn't do it. Get it? Now, and this is the most important part, are you correct in your belief? Is there something "good" about looking at pornography? Hopefully you answered "No, there is nothing good." Write down three of your own belief structures that make you vulnerable to temptation:

1) _____

2) _____

3) _____

The other mechanism that allows us to do un-Godly things is what psychologists call "permissive beliefs." As Christians, we can think of these structures as "Satan's Lies." Being vulnerable to temptation is only half of the problem. The other half of the problem has to do with how you can make it "OK" for you to do that which is against your own morality and value system. Here are some of the beliefs we learned gave us "permission" to act out our evil desires:

√ we "deserved" our treat for we had worked hard
√ no one would know
√ it is our body, and we weren't hurting anyone
√ we would only "just look", and not touch
√ we would only have coffee, just as friends

Some of us refer to these beliefs as "Satan's Lies." Write down three of Satan's Lies that make it OK for you to act out:

1) _____

2) _____

3) _____

God's Truth

"The weapons we fight with are not the weapons of the world. On the contrary, they have divine power to demolish strongholds. We demolish arguments and every pretension that sets itself up against the knowledge of God, and we take captive every thought to make it obedient to Christ."

— *2 Corinthians 10:4-5*

In 2 Corinthians 10:5, Paul writes that we are to "take captive every thought to make it obedient to Christ." Do you know how many thoughts you have in a day? A good auctioneer can throw out about 250 words in a minute. Your brain, at top speed, can generate about 2500 words in the same sixty seconds! Not that we do that all day long, but it gives you a perspective about how many thoughts you DO have in a day. Of those thousands of thoughts every day, how many do YOU "take captive?" That's what I thought.

Most of us don't take very many thoughts captive, and make them obedient to Christ. To "take captive" is a military term, it means to surround with an overwhelming force. Why do you think God instructed us to consider every single thought a mortal enemy until proven innocent? Because God knows how he made us – free will and all.

Therefore, if you truly want to be free, you must allow God to renew your mind. That which you used to believe was good, you must see through God's eyes, as the evil that it is. Remember, God has promised to help us with this process. It is not in and of ourselves, right? It is God IN us, changing us from the inside out.

Here are some of Satan's Lies that are countered by God's Truth:

Satan's Lie	God's Truth
• we can stop	• once we start, we can't stop
• no one would know	• God will know, I know
• we weren't hurting anyone	• it hurts us & those who care about us

Write down three of God's Truths that counter the three Satan's Lies you wrote down previously:

1) _____

_____

_____

2) _____

_____

_____

3) _____

_____

_____

Repentance

"Repentance...is recoil, recoil not from the bad act and it's painful consequences, but from the principle underlying the act."

— *Felix Adler*

Now that you realize the "principle underlying" your acting out, you are in a position to repent. Many pastors define repentance as to "turn and walk away" from. It is hard to walk away from something you don't know and understand. If, for example, I tell you to turn and walk away from the fliberrtygibbet in the room with you, but you don't know what that is, you wouldn't know which way to turn, would you? But if I ask you to turn and walk away from the sofa, you'll likely be able to do that fairly easily, assuming you know what a sofa is.

Repentance is not a synonym for "remorse", or to "feel badly" about our behaviors. Many of us mistakenly believed that we only truly repented when we have sufficiently self-flagellated ourselves so that we bled profusely from multiple wounds (metaphorically speaking). Of course, remorse is a required component of true repentance, but it is not sufficient, in and of itself. The Greek word for repentance is best translated as a "change of understanding" about a thing. In other words, when we repent of a thing we are saying that we no longer believe the same way about the thing. We have had a significant change in our belief structures. Interestingly enough, when these changes in beliefs happen, we find ourselves notably immune to temptations – these things are no longer "good ideas" as they once were to us.

Our friend Bob can help us understand this concept as it expressed itself in his life. At one point in time, Bob greatly enjoyed his relationships with dancers at strip bars and found this activity to be a very "good idea". At another time, he began to see the emptiness in the activity – that the girls didn't really care about him, only about his money. With that change of perspective, he no longer saw going to the strip club as a good idea and he was able to choose to turn his back on the behavior and walk away. He had truly repented by making a change in his beliefs, which resulted in a change of behavior. There is no repentance where there is no change in behavior and beliefs.

An interesting side note is that no amount of beating himself up for his acting out behaviors had ever resulted in a lasting change in his acting out. Making yourself feel bad about something usually only leads to more acting out, which leads to beating yourself up more, which leads to more acting out, and so on. However a change of belief can lead to a genuine change of direction.

As we read in "The Problem," lust has always been there for us. When other people let us down, disappoint us, or abandon us, lust always answered our call. Even though it later leaves us broken, alone, and bleeding by the side of the road, we still call on it time after time after time. In order for us to "de-throne" lust, and truly give our lives to Christ, we first have to surrender our "right" to lust. God will not take that away from us. We must lay it at His feet, voluntarily, time after time, after time.

1) How long have you had a relationship with lust?_____

2) Describe your first memory of lusting. _____

_____
_____
_____
_____
_____

3) What might happen inside you if you give up your right to have an ongoing relationship with lust? _____

_____
_____
_____
_____
_____

4) What is in the way for you to surrender your right to lust? _____

_____
_____
_____
_____
_____

5) A principle of human functioning is that we tend to hang on to "what we've got" until we get "something better" to replace it. Are you willing to choose to surrender your right to lust and replace that with trust in Jesus? _____

_____
_____
_____
_____

    If you answered "YES" to number 5, above, then take a moment now to say this prayer:

    "Lord Jesus, I realize that I have been indulging my lust and that it is only your Love which will make me whole. I do hereby surrender my right to lust and ask that you fill me with your perfect love."

6) Look up the following verses in your Bible; write them in the space provided, and then write down what that verse means to you and your Third Step.

    Verse   Meaning

Romans 3:22 _____

_____

_____

Proverbs 3:5-6 _____

_____

_____

2 Corinthians 5:17 _____

_____

_____

Matthew 11:28-30_____

_____

_____

Phillippians 1:6_____

_____

_____

A Daily Walk

"Trust in the LORD with all your heart and lean not on your own understanding; in all your ways acknowledge him, and he will make your paths straight."

— Proverbs 3: 5-6

Turning your life and will over to God is not something you do one time. It is something you do every single day, sometimes second-by-second. Remember, it is not a miracle or a magic pill. It is simply choosing His will, and not our own.

One final aspect of turning our will over to God is the requirement to be in an active relationship with Him. After all, how can you turn your will over to God, if you don't know what His will is? The way we learn God's will is to practice a skill relatively new to most of us – listening. We learn how to listen to His voice as we read His Word. We learn how to listen to Him through the voices of others – our pastor, our mentors, sponsors and others. We learn how to hear His Holy Spirit as we pray. As David writes in the Psalms, God tells us to:

"Be still, and know that I am God…"
— Psalms 46:10

For many of us, turning our lives over to God is a frightening thing. Part of that may be our fear of the unknown – in that it is something we have never done before. Or perhaps it is a fear of the "known" in the sense of what we imagine it will mean based on what we have heard from preachers or other Christians. What if God decides to make us be missionaries to some tribe of headhunters in deepest, darkest Africa, or something like that? They cut people's heads off there, you know!

For those of us who have faced that fear and dared to trust God completely with our lives, we can only encourage you that God is NOT a capricious tyrant who couldn't care less about what you want. He is a loving father, who finds His greatest joy in our happiness. And because He made you, only He knows best what will make you truly happy.

Begin to commit yourself to a couple of disciplines starting today: 1) commit to a daily quiet time of reading His Word and prayer, and 2) commit to a "life-style" of open prayer with Him throughout the day. Sometimes a daily devotional is one of the best parts of the day. We recommend that we set the tone for the day by beginning our day with our "quiet time" with the Lord. If you are not a morning person, or cannot make the time available in the morning, we suggest finding at least four or five minutes to connect with ourselves and with Him in a brief reading, meditation and prayer. Later in the day, at lunch, or before bed, we make time for a longer time of study in the Word. If we are participating in a formal Bible study, then that activity will provide structure for our time. There are many excellent Bible studies available, and we provide a few recommended topical studies in our Bibliography (many of which can be purchased through our online store at www.rsaministries.org - a portion of your purchase will go to support our ministry).

Step Four

We made a searching and fearless moral inventory of ourselves.

> *"It is not the lie that passeth through the mind, but the lie that sinketh in, and settleth in it, that doth the hurt."*
>
> *— Francis Bacon*

Sharon set her coffee cup back down and considered her new sponsor, Karan. "Mid 40's I think," Sharon thought to herself. "Not old enough to be my mother, but old enough, evidently, to think she knows something."

Speaking up rather suddenly, Karan said, "You're still not sure about this step study thing, are you, Sharon?"

She replied, "Well, no, not really. Especially Step Four. I don't see how writing down everything we've ever done wrong plus all of our resentments will make anything any better."

Karan smiled and took a sip of her own coffee, "I can tell you what my sponsor told me when I said the same thing to her. 'You don't have to understand for it to work, you just have to be willing.'"

Sharon screwed up her face, "What does that mean?" she said.

Karan laughed, "Yea, that's what I said, too!"

Not laughing, Sharon said, "You're really not being all that helpful right now Miss Sponsor," with a bite of sarcasm in her voice.

Without loosing any of her smile, Karan replied, "Oh, I see how it is with you, Sharon. You want everything to make perfect sense so it fits into nice neat little boxes for you." Now she let the smile fade from her face and a seriousness overtake it, "Ok, fine, here you go: It is the 'wrongness' in our past that continues to create 'wrongness' in our present. Whether it is the wrongs we've done to others, or the wrongs done to us, the damage has screwed us over and there's only one way to heal: We have to deal with it all."

In Step Three we examined our long standing relationship with lust and our right, as free-will beings, to choose to lust. In the end we made a decision to turn our will and our lives over to God's care, and to repeat that step as many times a day as necessary to maintain our sobriety. In Steps Four through Ten we will work at doing what the leopard cannot do, change our "spots." We have learned that sex is not the problem; it is only a symptom of a deeper and more serious illness in the "core" of our hearts, which distorts our view of the world and ourselves. It sustains our "stinking thinking" in all of its varied and subtle ways. In Step 4 we start this process of allowing God to change our character defects into character assets by conducting a fearless, moral inventory.

The first paragraph of "Chapter Five – How It Works" in the Big Book of AA introduces Step Four this way:

> *"Rarely have we seen a person fail who has thoroughly followed our path. Those who do not recover are people who cannot or will not completely give themselves to*

this simple program, usually men or women who are constitutionally incapable of being honest with themselves. There are such unfortunates. They are not at fault; they seem to have been born that way. They are naturally incapable of grasping and developing a manner of living which demands rigorous honesty. Their chances are less than average...but many of them do recover if they have the capacity to be honest."

- A.A. World Services

Most of us wondered if we had completely lost the capacity to be honest with ourselves — we had been lying for so long. We have lied to others, to God (as if that's really possible), and to ourselves. Were we one of the "unfortunates"? The idea almost overwhelmed us to the point of giving up. However, we also realized that we were more afraid of continuing in our addiction than we were of trying as best we could to learn to be honest.

To make our addiction work, we had to indulge our rationalizations and denials. To make recovery work, we have to face the ugly truth of who we have become: liars, cheaters, thieves, and more. It is only by being honest about who we are at this moment, that we can make a change by standing on the solid ground of truth.

Bob had struggled for weeks to start his fourth step. He had experienced a sense of relief, and something like a new beginning when he completed his third step. Making the decision to turn his life over to God lifted a heavy, invisible burden from his shoulders. However now, to turn away from that bright future into his painful past was NOT something he looked forward to.

Step Four asks us to take a "...fearless moral inventory." That means we take a brutally honest look at ourselves. If we allow our fear of what we might see limit or distort our work, we know we would not reach sobriety. The certainty of where we would go back to made our fears of facing our ugliness fade away. So we chose honesty, and sought integrity.

Morality

"Morality, concerned with bringing human activity into conformity with God's will, has a bearing on everything that touches human rights and duties."

— *Catholic Bishops of the U.S., November 1951*

According to Webster, morals are the manners or customs that relate to, or deal with the distinction between right and wrong in conduct. They are the rules, or standards that we each believe in to guide our behavior and that of others. The degree to which we behave consistently with our own morals is an indicator of our personal integrity. When we fail to live by or own standards on a consistent basis, we call that a "character defect."

To conduct a moral inventory, we must take "stock" of our character defects, or areas of our behavior patterns, where we are not living consistent with our morals. We have to be honest with ourselves about the harms we have done to others. In recovery, we have learned that resentments and fears are a trigger for our acting out. We had to learn how to deal with our resentments and fears, so that we could stop acting out. In a sense, we were never "free" from our addiction until we had been freed of our triggers.

There is only one little problem with taking our own inventory: We have to be able, and willing to be totally honest with ourselves. Well, as they say, "De-Nile is not just a river in Egypt!" Most of us have used our fears and resentments to justify our behaviors. As long as we see our behaviors through the filter of rationalizations, we won't see anything "wrong" with our behaviors. That would make for a very short inventory! The wisdom of our program has taught us that the first thing we have to do, is to deal with all of our resentments and fears, before we can be honest with ourselves about the harms we have done to others.

Resentments

"Many a person seems to think it isn't enough for the government to guarantee him the pursuit of happiness. He insists it also run interference for him."

— *Anonymous*

A resentment is a feeling of deep anger and ill-will. Sometimes it is a sense that someone "owes" us something. We have resentments when we blame someone else for how we are feeling or behaving. We believe they purposefully wronged us in some way that we cannot excuse. How do you know if you have resentments against someone? Well, if you can't, or don't want to face someone you have had a relationship with, then it just might be a resentment that is in your way.

We can resent people, places, institutions, and things. Many of us found we had resentments against: mothers, fathers, sisters, brothers, aunts, uncles, grandparents, cousins, spouses, ex-spouses, friends, ex-friends, neighbors, ex-neighbors, bosses, co-workers, supervisors, administrators, teachers, executives, lawyers, judges, police, cell-mates, janitors, store clerks, pastors, preachers, doctors, Sunday-school teachers, coaches, assistant coaches, customers, presidents, kings, queens, popes, nuns, churches, the IRS, hospitals, meetings, rules, laws, regulations, policies & procedures, suggestions, demands, limitations of any kind, expectations of any kind, gravity, age, time, romance novels, cars, not-having-a-car, Rubik's-stupid-Cube, non-magic 8 Balls, and many more things.

One way to think of resentments is as someone or something that has interfered with us in some way, perhaps in our ambitions, our security, our self-esteem, or our relationships. For your Fourth Step, you will need a pad of paper, or a journal, and a pen or pencil. That is the old school way. For you "new school" folks, you'll need your computer and your software of choice. Start by making five columns: the first is for the "whos and whats" we are resentful of; the second is for the reason we are resentful; and the third is how it affected us. Leave the fourth and fifth blank for now.

First, we must make a list of all of the resentments we have. This part of our process may take several days or even weeks. At first, many of us insisted we have few, if any, resentments. But as we started to write down the few that came to mind, more followed closely behind.

Next, we need to ask ourselves why we are angry or resentful. For every person, place, or thing on your list, write down a few words about why you are angry or resentful. Be as specific as possible. We learn from specifics, not generalities. For example, we learn only a little from "he stole from me," and we learn a great deal from, "he stole MY

CAR from me."

The program teaches us that if we are disturbed by something, no matter what the cause, there is now something the matter with me. In order to understand why we are resentful or angry, we have to understand how the event impacted (or disturbed) us. Did it affect my self-esteem? Perhaps it affected my finances? Or, it may have affected my ambition, my personal relationships, or my sexual relationships. In the third column, list the area or areas where you were impacted by the person, place, or thing of which you were resentful.

When Sharon got to this part of step four she first thought that she didn't have much to write. Her sponsor suggested that she begin writing from where ever she could remember and work from there. Soon, the memories started coming back fast, and furious. When she had trouble remembering certain things she found that she could talk to family members, friends who knew her during the time in question, or even play songs from that time of her life to help jog her memory. It was not long before she had quite a lengthy list going. In particular, she learned that much of her childhood sexuality, which she had always thought of as being by her choice, was actually abuse, and not her fault. Her sponsor encouraged her to begin some therapy work in addition to her step work.

Here is an example of what a resentment list looks like. For brevity's sake, we'll use abbreviations: self-esteem = S.E., sexual relations = S.R., and ambitions = well…see if you can figure it out.

I Am Resentful At	Because	Affects My
Spouse	Not enough sex.	S.E., S.R.
Older Brother	Said I was stupid.	Ambitions
Rubik's-Stupid-Cube	I couldn't solve it.	S.E.

Take some time now to begin working on your own list. It is best to approach the list as something you will work on over the next few days or weeks. Once you feel certain you have exhausted your memory, then take a "gentleness break" before you return to the work.

Welcome back! Now that you have listed and understood your resentments and how they affected you, you can look for mistakes of your own and learn from them. Title your fourth column, "My Mistakes." For each person, place, or thing listed, ask yourself, "What mistakes did I make in this situation?" "Was I selfish, self-centered, dishonest, prideful, greedy, lustful, envious, jealous, critical, or something else?" We must look hard for our own mistakes, ignoring our rationalizations about what others had done to us. For many of us, this was the first time we had actually become willing to take responsibility for our own actions.

Having trouble coming up with ideas about what you did wrong? Then find a couple of "safe people" whom you trust like a sponsor, mentor, accountability partner, or therapist, and ask for input from them. Ask them to give you "straightforward truth" as they see it. Your job will be to show them respect by taking notes about what they have to say, and by not arguing with them. Ask clarifying questions, but do not defend yourself.

Freedom

"...and through Him everyone who believes is freed from all things, from which you could not be freed through the Law of Moses."

— Acts 13:39

In recovery, we found that freedom from our addiction came from several phenomena. First, our minds had to be renewed from the "stinkin' thinkin'" that was our disease. Second, we needed to have a "spiritual awakening." Third, we had to learn how to be people of balance and integrity. Fourth, we had to learn about grace and forgiveness. Any one of those tasks is monumental. If we try to accomplish that of ourselves, we will surely fail. However, if we learn to "let go and let God" we find that the "indwelling" Holy Spirit transforms us.

In the Book of Acts, Chapter 13, verse 39, God's Word promises that through Christ we can be "...freed from all things, from which you could not be freed through the Law of Moses." The Law of Moses is the Ten Commandments. Do you remember those? Thou shalt not steal, Thou shalt not covet thy neighbor's wife, etc...? If you have ever lied, cheated, stolen, or lusted, you are a violator of the Law of Moses, and therefore a sinner and subject to sentencing under that law. Under the Law of Moses, there is only conviction; there is no Grace, no freedom. What is the magic elixir that makes us free? Simply put, it is forgiveness. Because of Christ's work on the cross for us, not only are we forgiven of our sins, but also we now have the power to forgive others for their sins against us! Christ paid for their sins, too.

Pull your Resentment List out again. Now we are going to complete the fifth column to our list. Entitle it, "New, Non-Resentful Perspective." Pick an item on the list that is relatively easy for you to deal with. Now say this prayer, "Lord Jesus, help me to see this event through your eyes. Please help me forgive this situation and let go of my resentment." Now re-examine your original resentment and try to look at it from God's perspective. We have learned that at the very least, we can see the person who wronged us as a "sick" person, just as we are sick. We then begin to pray for healing in their life. For example, we may have resentment against the man or woman we saw recently, whose manner of dress caused us to be tempted to lust. We are outraged that they would do something that would cause us to stumble. "How dare she dress that way at church!" we cry. We are offended in our self-esteem and perhaps even our sexual relations. As we ask the Lord to let us see her through His eyes, the visage of the seductress fades away and we see the truth of this woman whose self-esteem is so low she has to display her body to feel good about herself. We see her for the sick and wounded person that she is. Write that new, non-resentful perspective down. Here are some examples from our earlier list.

I Am Resentful At	Because	Affects My	New View
1) Spouse	Not enough sex.	S.E., S.R.	I'm not good at romancing her.
2) Older Brother	Said I was stupid.	Ambitions	He was hurting from our family too.

| 3) Rubik's-Stupid-Cube | I couldn't solve it. | S.E. | Nobody else I know solved it either. |

In the process of dealing with our resentments, we began to comprehend how destructive they had been in our lives. They made us intolerant, self-absorbed, selfish, impatient, self-righteous, and lacking in empathy for others. Most terribly, they created a wall between God and ourselves. When we refuse to forgive others, we reject God's forgiveness for us, which is to deny his very love for us. In our addiction, we declared we were right to hold onto our resentments, for we were god of our lives. We isolated ourselves from our God and our fellow man. Look to what ends our self-service had brought us? – demoralization, dehumanization, and deterioration. In our recovery, we began to realize the futility of our resentments. By letting go of our resentments, we are learning forgiveness, tolerance, patience, empathy, and good will towards all – even our enemies. We are restoring our relationship with God and our relatedness with our fellow man.

Fears

"For I know the plans I have for you," declares the LORD, "plans to prosper you and not to harm you, plans to give you hope and a future."

— *-Jeremiah 29:11*

For many of us, our fears were as much a trigger for our acting out, as were our resentments. Therefore, we needed to do the same work for our fears, as we did for our resentments. We started by making a list of our fears, and then we asked ourselves why we had them.

What were we afraid of? Many of us have been afraid of lots of things: failure, success, rejection, ridicule, appearing imperfect or looking stupid, people, the future, death, sexuality, spiders, snakes, roaches, mice, other creepy crawlies, high places, closed spaces, dark spaces, open spaces, not having a job, having a job, change, confrontation, women, men, children, malls, stores, theaters, theme parks, parties, family gatherings, responsibility, loss of control, the police, God, mom, dad, grandma, grandpa, aunts, uncles, neighbors, tests, expectations, and many, many more. Write down all the things you can think of that have elicited that reaction inside of you during your life. For most of us, we feared because our self-reliance failed us. Deep inside some part of us that felt inadequate welled up, and caused the ground beneath our feet to be unsteady. Fear is simply the emotion that signaled the loss of our confidence.

Some have said that the presence of fear is due to the absence of trust. We might lack trust in ourselves, in someone else, or in God. For example, if we are afraid of a snake, it is because we lack the confidence (trust in ourselves) in our own competence to deal with or protect ourselves from the snake. There is an old story about the Great Wallenda who suspended a tight rope across Niagra Falls. There were crowds on both the U.S. and Canadian sides cheering him on. No body had ever walked a tight rope across the falls before, and he wasn't using a safety harness. Any slip would lead to his certain death. Carefully, he made his first crossing and the crowds cheered wildly. Unbelieveably, he crossed back again! The crowds cheered even louder. Then he rode a bicycle back and forth! Everyone marveled at his daring feat, laughing in death's face. Finally, he put a wheelbarrow on the tightwire, loaded with weights, and crossed back yet again. This time, he asked the crowd, "Who thinks I can put a man in this wheelbarrow and safely wheel him across the wire?" The crowd cheered loudly in affirmation. The Great Wallenda asked the crowd, "Great! Who wants to ride?" The crowd fell silent. This is the difference between believing about something and believing in something. If you truly trust, you get in the wheelbarrow!

In Step Three we made a decision to turn our lives and our wills over to the care of God. In practice, we learned that trusting an infinite God, was much more secure than trusting exceedingly finite beings. In His Word He promises to take care of us, as a Shepherd cares for his flock. If we choose to trust in His plan for our lives, we can learn to be less fearful. For each of the items on your list of fears, ask yourself, "Why did I have this fear?" Then write how you can give that fear to God and trust His plan for your life rather than in trusting in yourself. For example, if I have a fear of not getting a job that I am scheduled to interview for, I can turn the fear into trust by choosing to believe that God has a plan for my life that includes what job I have, and when I get it. This is not a fatalistic, "Que sera, sera" attitude (whatever will be, will be). This is trust in God's character.

Sexual Relations

"The body of a sensualist is the coffin of a dead soul."

— Christian Nestell Bovee

For many of us, the task of writing down all of our sexual relations is literally impossible. We simply do not remember every single event. So we rely on the guidance of the Holy Spirit and commit this work to God's care. Through God's prompting, we will be able to remember every event that He knows we need to deal with. Before starting your list, pray this prayer, "Lord Jesus, I invite your Holy Spirit to come and minister to my memory, to bring to my mind any and all of my sexual behaviors which you need me to address."

We found that we could benefit from the work we began in Step One with our Addiction History Timeline. Pull out your Step One notebook and review your addiction timeline. Use that as a rough framework for recreating every event, starting from your first sexual memory and ending with your last sexual experience. Yes that includes EVERY sexual event: sex with others, sex with self, or just indulging lust. Yes, that will be a long list!

You will need to make three columns for this work. The first column is labeled "Sexual Behaviors." The second column is for analyzing the nature of each of those behaviors and is labeled "Addictive?" The third column is called "Repentance." In the second column, you will indicate which events were addictive in nature and which were "normal." To differentiate between addictive and normal, ask yourself this question, "In this event was my sexuality lust-based and self-serving, or was it love-based and other-serving?" Many of us looked at this difference and laughed, we've never known sex as "love-based and other-serving!" In that event, this part of the work will go quickly! We asked ourselves when was our sex abusive to ourselves, or others? When was it demoralizing or dehumanizing? When did we manipulate, coerce, or force a person or a situation to get what we wanted? That includes coercing someone to engage in a behavior with which he or she was not comfortable. When did our sexual relations involve the direct or indirect payment for sexual services? When did we allow ourselves to be taken advantage of, or participate in a behavior with which we were not comfortable? When did we steal time from others to indulge our lust? For example, missing a business meeting because we were at the strip club, or missing dinner with our family to indulge a rendezvous with our sex partner. As we worked our way through our list we began to see how many ways our addiction had violated our own boundaries, in addition to the boundaries of those who participated with us.

In facing the truth about our sexual indulgences, we learned several things. We came to understand the meaning of the term "demoralized" in a new way. We realized that when we violated our own morals, even though we convinced ourselves we didn't believe in them, that we destroyed a part of ourselves. We also began to comprehend how much our lust had become the center of our life, and how much we had come to depend on lust rather than God. Finally, we realized how much of a liar lust was. It had promised to build us up and make us whole. Instead, it had, slowly and surely, destroyed our lives and our character. We were disgusted with the truth of who we had become.

Repentance

"Most people repent their sins by thanking God they ain't so wicked as their neighbors."

— Josh Billings

We were finally able to see ourselves clearly when we had thrown away the lies of the Enemy that had distorted our view of ourselves and others. At last, we reached a place where true repentance could accomplish its healing work in our hearts, rather than the lip service we had paid in the past. Luke writes there is more rejoicing in heaven over one sinner who repents than there is over 99 people who do not need to repent (Luke 15:7). Imagine that, when we repent, the angels throw a party in heaven! In the midst of this deep work we are overwhelmed with our own shame and guilt. Once we have repented, we have to accept God's grace that we are forgiven. "Grace" is defined as "unmerited favor," meaning that we get something positive that we do not deserve. How true, how true! We do not deserve the forgiveness of God and of others for our mistakes and miseries. However, His forgiveness is there, nonetheless.

In the last column we simply need to do our "repentance work." Repentance work is confessing our sin to God, expressing our remorse for the sin, giving up our right to continue in that behavior, and asking His forgiveness for the sin. That's all there is to it! Then we mark the item with a cross, to symbolize that the event is covered by the blood of Jesus and forgiven. That symbol reminds us to forgive ourselves.

A Fearless, Moral Inventory

> "Morality is not properly the doctrine how we make ourselves happy, but how we make ourselves worthy of happiness."
>
> — Immanuel Kant

Now that we have faced the ugliness of our resentments, fears, and sexual behaviors, we are able to assess the condition of our position, relative to our moral standards. The time has come to take our moral inventory.

Review the following list of morals and rate yourself on a scale of 0 to 100% on how consistent your behaviors are with your morals. 100% would mean that you are one hundred percent consistent with your morals, and 0% would mean you are completely inconsistent. Alternately, you can translate the percentage into a standard grade according to the follow scale. Rate yourself first on each category as you see yourself in the past year, and then give yourself an overall, "lifetime" rating.
{0 – 59% = "F," 60 – 69% = "D," 70 – 79% = "C," 80 – 89% = "B," 90 – 100% = "A"}

AREA	RATING Past Year/Lifetime
Honesty (truthfulness)	____/____
Taxes	____/____
Money	____/____
Facts about self or events	____/____
Other	____/____
Sexual purity in Thoughts	____/____
Sexual purity in Behaviors	____/____
Self-centeredness (putting yourself or your needs ahead of others without appropriate reasons for doing so)	____/____
Gossiping	____/____
Keeping promises	____/____
Timeliness	____/____
Inappropriate behaviors	____/____
Indulging anger	____/____
Taking advantage of others	____/____
Manipulating people	____/____
Responsibility (paying bills on time, keeping appointments, meeting other life responsibilities as a father, husband, son, friend or other)	____/____

This list is not intended to be exhaustive, so take a few moments to think through other areas of morality in your life and give yourself a rating. Now that you have completed this rating, you can re-evaluate yourself every six months or once a year to keep yourself accountable to your moral standards.

For each of the above items where you scored a "B" or less during the past year, write down specific examples of when and where you have failed. Yes, as a Christian,

God calls us to make all "A's" on our moral report cards. You might note that you don't have to be "perfect" to get an "A." God doesn't expect us to be perfect, but He does expect us to work very hard at leading moral lives.

    Area   Grade   Specific Example

1)_____

2)_____

3)_____

4)_____

We mentioned earlier in this Guide that we had to learn how to be persons who lead balanced lives. Go back through the list and detail below the categories where you scored an "A." Take a few moments to thank God for the changes He has made in your life, or acknowledge the "strengths" of character you have. Come back and review this list whenever you work on your character weaknesses begins to bring on too much guilt and shame, or if you sense a lust-attack developing. Remember, as addicts, we have to battle that "all or nothing" thinking, which generates lies such as "I am completely bad so I may as well act out" or, "I'm a hopeless case, God can't or won't help me." God's Word promises us that He loves us just as we are, warts and all. We do not have to be perfect before He will love us. We are already forgiven! Take a moment now to write down your strength areas and some specific examples.

    Strength   Specific Example

1)_____

2)_____

3)_____

4)_____

5)_____

Now, put your paper down for one to two weeks and then come back and re-read your entire work. You will no doubt see things differently at that point. You may spot some things you missed, remembered some things you had forgotten, or found some obvious, "stinkin' thinking" right there on the page. If you do, re-work that part of your Fourth Step.

Having trouble coming up with strengths about yourself? This is another good opportunity to ask for feedback from a trustworthy, safe person – or two. Check with your sponsor, accountability partners, therapist, or other mentors. Get two or three opinions and remember, don't argue with them, just say, "Thank you."

Character

"Out of our beliefs are born deeds. Out of our deeds we form habits; out of our habits grow our characters; and on our character we build our destination."

— Henry Hancock

While morality is the standard by which we should behave, character is the measure of our ability to choose to behave according to those standards. Though Bob and Sharon still have a long way to go in their journey through the twelve steps, they, like most of us, have experienced a shift in the nature of their day-to-day lives. While they have "turned the corner" so to speak, they are not free from temptation, but they see themselves and their path through life so very differently that it is hard for them not to think and act differently every day. Each day, they allow the healing grace of Jesus to renew their minds, and that slow process of sanctification (becoming more like Christ) is bearing much fruit.

Congratulations! You have just completed your Fourth Step! You should be proud of yourself for the courage it took to deal with these issues. You will find that you have to return to your Fourth Step in the future, starting with Step Five, when you have to share it with someone else. You have begun the process of building a Godly character out of a godless chaos. That is a process we continue every single day by choosing to live in accordance with God's standards for our lives. We are free indeed!

"So if the Son sets you free, you will be free indeed."

— John 8:36

Step Five

Admitted to God, to ourselves, and to another human being the exact nature of our wrongs.

"The confession of evil works is the first beginning of good works."

— Saint Augustine

"But WHY do I have to share my fourth step with you? What good will it do?" Sharon asked her sponsor, Karan. "I mean, why would you, or anyone, even want to hear it?"

Karan looked at her with a slight smile and said, "Sharon, why do you think we need to share our fourth step?"

"I have no idea!" Sharon retorted. "That's why I'm asking you! You're supposed to be the know-it-all-sponsor!"

"Not a good enough effort," said Karan firmly, "Try again."

Sharon glared at Karan in stony silence and Karan let her sit in it for a long couple of minutes.

Finally Karan prodded, "How about you think about why the idea of sharing your fourth step with me, or *anyone* for that matter, is so upsetting to you?"

Sharon looked down at the table and let out a loud breath as she said, "Because I'm embarrassed and ashamed of the things I've done...of who I am."

"Of who you were," corrected Karan.

Step Five is about confession, and also about integrity. For some of us this was the first time in our lives we had the strength of character to be brutally honest with ourselves, with God, and another human being about the depths of depravity our insanity had taken us to. And if we dare to be continually honest with ourselves, it will not be the last.

Why is it difficult for us to admit our mistakes? It is because confession requires us to confront our own evil. Acknowledging our wrongs in writing our Fourth Step awakens our conscience, which had been lulled to sleep by our denial. Many of us found this process to be both painful and freeing. Some bit of peace had begun to creep into our troubled minds. The Fourth Step sparked something that may grow and flourish, but only if we continue to practice honesty with ourselves and others.

Step Five, admitting to God and to another human, the exact nature of our wrongs, is the first step in taking responsibility for our past actions. That action is the first step in changing our future, our first opportunity to choose to be different. It seems so hard to somehow become different than we were. We were liars, and we must become people of honesty. We were thieves, and we must become people of charity. We were cheaters, and we must become people of integrity. We must choose to face life truthfully, and accept it on its own terms. We can no longer take what doesn't belong to us, or use others to gain for ourselves. We must pack away our cape, and learn to walk like everyone else, instead of trying to fly. The first step towards our recovery begins with accepting our own humanity.

Facing our sins created, in some of us, disturbing emotions. Others of us have not yet had our conscience awakened enough to feel anything significant about our past. Or, perhaps we still have justifications or rationalizations for our behaviors, or have not sufficiently dealt with our resentments. The wisdom of our program taught us that this would come to us in time, as we earnestly work our program of recovery.

We thought that Step Four was the "hard" part, until we realized that we had to share all of our darkness with another person in Step Five. Some of us experienced this as anxiety or fear, and others found their minds filled with excuses or distractions.

What obstacles do you have (fears, excuses, distractions) to doing a Fifth Step? ___
_____
_____
_____
_____
_____
_____

In Program, we hear that we have to become willing to go to "whatever lengths are necessary to get and stay sober." What are you willing to do to work through your obstacles to doing the Fifth Step? Take each obstacle you wrote about above, and write an action step(s) here. _____
_____
_____
_____
_____

Admitted to God...

> *"If we confess our sins, he is faithful and just and will forgive us our sins and purify us from all unrighteousness."*
>
> — 1 John 1:9

Step Five also requires us to deal with our issues about God. Some of us may still carry some anger, or resentment against God, for example, and therefore be reluctant to talk to Him. Some of us had significant problems with this step. We did not believe ourselves to be worthy of forgiveness, and therefore saw no point in confession to God. If you have any such obstacles about admitting your wrongs to God, and you did not list them above, take a moment to write them down, and then write down your action step(s) for each obstacle.

Those who have walked the road of sobriety ahead of us have instructed us to "lead with the body and the mind/heart will follow". They told us that there is good news and bad news in recovery: The good news is you get your feelings back; the bad news is you get your feelings back! Part of the goal of Step Five is to help us to begin to reconnect with God. We have learned that in order to connect with God, we must first connect with ourselves. Some of us haven't connected with our feelings to any significant degree yet and that will make this work a predominantly intellectual effort. Others of us, however, have begun to get our feelings back and may find these strong negative emotions generating a strong urge to run in the opposite direction. If that is true for you, then the strength and encouragement of your support network is critical in assisting you to walk through these uncomfortable feelings. Remember, program also teaches us that, even when it comes to unpleasant emotions, "this too, shall pass".

My obstacles to confessing my sins to God: _____

_____
_____
_____
_____
_____
_____
_____

What am I willing to do about them? My action step(s): _____

_____
_____
_____
_____
_____
_____
_____

Now that you are ready to admit your wrongs to God, how are you going to do that? It is very important to make adequate time for yourself to do this part of Step Five, and very easy to overlook it. We recommend that you schedule multiple "appointments" with God to work this through. The first session or two is to go through your Fourth Step with Him. The last session is to go back through it a second time. For some of us, this second run-through is necessary to better receive the forgiveness that He promises. The second run-through also gives us a different perspective on this experience, and allows us a chance to catch any part of the experience we missed the first time.

...to ourselves...

> *"When pride comes, then comes disgrace, but with humility comes wisdom."*
>
> *— Proverbs 11:2*

To a degree, we have admitted the nature of our wrongs in our work through Steps One through Four. We have admitted that we have a disease, that we need help, and that God is able to help us. Now we must admit to ourselves the exact nature of our wrongs. If we do not, we will remain in denial, and be unable to grow personally and spiritually. In preparing to share our Fourth Step with someone else, we should re-read it again, and press ourselves to be "brutally honest" with ourselves. Did we miss anything that we need to add or rework? If that is the case, then do it now before proceeding.

After weeks and weeks of inaction, Sharon's sponsor finally gave her an ultimatum: Work your fifth step or find a new sponsor. Sometimes "tough love" is the best kind. Reluctantly, Sharon agreed and asked what she needed to do. Her sponsor told her to ask God to give her courage to face her fears and then to re-read her fourth step. After that, they would meet so she could share it with her. Sharon finally submitted her right to avoid her own feelings and knelt before God. "Lord," she prayed, "I am terrified to share my past in all its fullness with Karan, please give me courage to do it afraid." She felt a sudden peace replace her dread, and she picked up her notebook and began to read.

...and to another human being...

> *"Therefore confess your sins to each other*
> *and pray for each other so that you may be healed.*
> *The prayer of a righteous man is powerful and effective."*
>
> *— James 5:16*

Ah, this is the moment that makes us anxious as no other. Most of us have never been totally honest about anything, much less everything, with someone else. But those who came before us in recovery tell us that there is healing in confession done in this way, with a safe person. Therefore, we take a deep breath, and take the risk. In so doing, we begin to realize at a deep level that we are not alone, and that we are loved. This is where we are finally able to choose to join the human race, and be at peace with our selves and our fellow man.

Sharon finally set an appointment to share her fourth step with Karan. Walking from her car, Sharon felt nauseous and had to keep reminding herself that this wasn't going to kill her. Karan welcomed her with a big hug, a cup of hot tea, and the reassurance that she would get through it all right. They sat down together and Karan opened in a short prayer, "Lord Jesus, I thank you for my sister, Sharon, and the great work that you have begun in her life. I ask for your comfort and your guidance as we work tonight, and may all the glory be yours. Amen." Karan asked Sharon to talk her way through her fourth step, rather than to just read it aloud. She told her to take her time, they were in no hurry, and could take breaks as needed. Sharon opened her notebook and began to tell her story. Three hours later they decided to call it an evening and to continue another night. Sharon could not believe how exhausted she was, and how curiously peaceful she felt.

...the exact nature of our wrongs.

The defining phrase in Step Five is "exact nature." We cannot soft-pedal these truths to ourselves. We must be exact, or specific, and we must take the time to think through the nature, or meaning, of our wrongs. For example, if I have to confess that I misrepresented to my significant other, my whereabouts on a particular night, I am not being specific about the event. Step Five requires us to be specific. The "exact" truth is that I did not "misrepresent" my whereabouts; I lied about it. The second part of this task is to specify the nature of this lie. In this example, the nature of the lie is betrayal. I betrayed the trust given to me by my significant other by lying about my whereabouts. I demonstrated that I am not trustworthy, that my "yes" is not necessarily yes, and my "no" is not necessarily no. This is what it means to admit the "exact nature" of our wrongs.

Doing your Fifth Step is both a simple and a difficult thing. You need to share your Fourth Step with another human being. Some people bring creative definitions to that term, so, for the sake of clarity's we specify that the person you share with must be alive, conscious, of reasonably sound mind, listening to you only, and able to fluently understand the language you choose to speak in. Additionally, and despite what some assert to the contrary, dogs and cats are not people, and do not count for this exercise.

Fifth Step Guidelines

The following are additional guidelines offered to assist you in working your Fifth Step.

☑ Prayerfully and carefully select the person(s) with whom you will be sharing your Fifth Step. Select only those who are "safe," and who will be supportive of your work. Some suggested people include accountability partners and sponsors. These are the preferred people; because they are in a unique position to do more than just listen. They may be able to give you some helpful and supportive feedback about your work.

☑ Carefully select the place where you will share your Fifth Step. This work may bring up some emotions for you, so it is best to have a quiet, private place (your friendly, neighborhood burger joint does not fit this definition).

☑ Schedule the time and place with the person. It is recommended that you reserve at least a couple of hours for this process, and take breaks as needed. Many people need more than one session to cover everything in their Fifth Step.

☑ Pray ahead of time for yourself, the meeting and for the person with whom you will be sharing. Ask the Holy Spirit to bring any additional areas or issues for you to light.

☑ When sharing, reveal the level of detail necessary to provide an adequate accounting of the "exact nature" of your wrongs, but not enough to cause your listener to stumble. For example, sharing that you have committed adultery is too vague, but sharing that you have had three extramarital affairs and that each lasted 6 months is specific enough. You can always ask your listener to give you feedback about how much detail they think you need to share on a specific issue.

☑ Remember to protect the privacy of any other persons with whom you were involved. This Fifth Step is about your character defects, not someone else's. Work your own program and let them work theirs.

☑ Bring your Fourth Step notes. Don't try to do this out of your head. Take this step seriously.

☑ Keep in mind that the goal is to recognize what you are responsible for, and to differentiate those things for which you are not responsible. For example, you are responsible if you coerced another person into sex with you, but you are not responsible if you were coerced into sex when you were a child.

☑ Pray afterward, for yourself, and for God's healing where it is needed.

Remember that this session may evoke many emotions, many of which have served as triggers. Therefore, make sure to plan appropriately for yourself for after the meeting. Make sure you have activated enough of your sober support network to help you process your "after-my-Fifth-step-feelings." Some of us have to avoid being alone after these sessions to keep us from falling into temptation. Others of us do better if we go spend even more time alone in prayer and meditation before the Lord. Seek the wisdom of those who know you best about what path your "after Step Five" should take.

What follows is a sample "List of Wrongs" to illustrate one way that you can work this part of Step Five.

My List of Wrongs (Sample)

Event or Wrong I Committed	The Nature of the Wrong
1) Extramarital affair w/co-worker. Lasted 6 months.	1) cheated on my wife, betrayed her trust, betrayed the trust of our family and friends, ruined her self-esteem.
2) stole time from work to indulge affair.	2) stealing, taking what isn't mine to take
3) stole time from family to indulge affair.	3) stealing, taking what isn't mine to take
4) lied to wife, friends, boss, and co-workers.	4) lying, dishonest, lack of integrity

5) lied to myself about the damage I was doing to everybody.	5) self-deception

The following chart provides a place for you to begin working your Fifth Step. Yes, most of us have to use more than one piece of paper to write out all of our wrongs and the nature of those wrongs. We just wanted to give you some space to get started. No, you can't stop at only one page…sorry. You may be surprised at how long it can take to reconstruct a lifetime of wrongs. Unless, perhaps you are like my grandfather who used to tell me, "You know, I was wrong once…then I found out I was mistaken!"

My List of Wrongs (for you to fill out)

Event or Wrong I Committed	The Nature of the Wrong

Step Six

We were entirely ready to have God remove all these defects of character.

> "Nothing spoils a confession like repentance."
>
> — Anatole France

Bob never really thought of himself as a dishonest person, except for the obvious lies he told about where he was or what he was doing at specific times. One night at their regular after-meeting-coffee, his sponsor, Dwight, confronted him about his lack of honesty.

"What do you mean saying I'm 'dishonest'?" Bob challenged to Dwight.

"Seriously, you think you're an 'honest' guy?" Dwight responded.

"How about you tell me what makes you think I'm **not**" said Bob.

"A better idea," fired back Dwight, "is you explain to me how 'honesty' includes being vague about when you're going to get home."

"Hey, I'm not a kid anymore," reasoned Bob. "I shouldn't have to answer to anybody."

"Oh really?" said Dwight. "First of all, when you trashed the trust of your wife, your family, your friends, and your employer, by lying and deceiving them about what you were doing with your time, you forfeited your right to enjoy their implicit trust in your use of your time. Secondly, an honest man does not live his life in the shadows, keeping parts of himself, even his time, secret from the most important people in his life. Unless, that is, you have something to hide."

A long and considered pause and Bob said, "Ahm, no...no, I don't have anything to hide, I guess you're right, Dwight. I'm having a hard time being willing to give up my selfishness. I want to do what I want to do when I want to do it."

"Excellent," encouraged Dwight. "Now you're ready to begin working on being **entirely** ready for God to do His thing with that selfishness."

...were entirely ready...

Most of us had to have it pointed out to us that being "ready" is not the same thing as being "entirely ready". A big, "Thank You!" to our sponsors for keeping us on our toes. What is the significance of the qualifier, "entirely"? It seems likely that it is a point of emphasis from one addict to another, knowing how we tend to hedge every bet, so that we would hold nothing back from God's character reconstruction work upon us. How do we become entirely ready? That's what Step Six is all about.

Step Five is about confession. Step Six is about repentance. The Greek word, "repentance," in the New Testament is "metanoia," which means "to have another mind" in regards to sin. It refers to a voluntary 'turning away' from sinful pursuits, in favor of a more Godly existence. Our character defects have led us down roads that brought chaos and destruction to our lives. We believed we could control lust, or that we were entitled to indulge it, or could take it only so far. These beliefs about our selves and others must be transformed, if we are to be truly sober and capable of living a sane life. The alternative is to continue the insane life of our addict. This is a journey, not an event. It is a way of living our life in humility and grace, instead of pride and arrogance.

It is interesting to note that in the New Testament, repentance is presented as one side of a coin, and faith as the other. Consider Paul's words from Acts (20:21):

> *"I have declared to both Jews and Greeks that they must turn to God in repentance and have faith in our Lord Jesus."*

Why does Paul make the point that repentance must be paired with faith? The answer has to do with the nature of the goal of repentance: forgiveness. We repent not just to change our behaviors, but also to seek reconciliation from others. Forgiveness is impossible without faith, because who can truly forgive sin, but God? Therefore, repentance is dependent upon faith in Jesus' work on the cross.

The Gospel of Mark tells us the story of a man who was paralyzed, but who had four friends who wanted to get him close to Jesus so that He could heal him. The crowd, however, was so large that they could not get him into the house where Jesus was teaching. Therefore, they went up on the roof, made a hole in it, and lowered him to the room below. Jesus saw their efforts as evidence of their faith and because of that, said to the paralytic, "Son your sins are forgiven." Some teachers of the law wondered to themselves, "Who can forgive sins but God alone?" Jesus answered them, "Which is easier to say to this paralytic, 'Your sins are forgiven,' or to say, 'Get up, take your mat and walk?' But that you may know that the Son of Man has authority on earth to forgive sins..." He said to the paralytic, "I tell you, get up, take your mat and go home." Mark tells us that the paralytic did just that, "...in full view of them all." (Mark 2:1-12). This account assures us that Jesus does have the power to forgive sins. If we have enough faith to allow Him to, He will not only forgive all of our sins, He will also heal our paralyzed hearts.

Repentance and faith are both a response to grace. Grace is defined as "unmerited favor" or being released from a sentence we deserve. Repentance means to change your ways of thinking and living. Faith is the belief that Jesus of Nazareth is the Son of God, who died on the cross for your sins, and who rose again in triumphant defeat of death. His death served as the atonement for all of our sins. The point of repentance and faith in response to grace is for the individual to accept forgiveness for his or her transgressions. Who among us deserves forgiveness? Right: No one; and who among us needs forgiveness? Right: Everyone.

Here is an uncommon story of grace in the lives of two men. In 1979 Kevin Koch was a 20-year-old major league hopeful, who took a job as a team's mascot after he realized he was not going to make it into the majors on his baseball talent. Although he he was unable to realize his childhood dreams of playing ball on the big stage, he was able to perform at the games, and gradually, he became friends with the athletes. In time, they let him in the "inner circle" and let him snort cocaine with them. Soon after that, the players were asking him to get the drug for them. Kevin's fame as the Pittsburgh Pirate's Parrot rose to the national level and he soon found himself one of baseball's most famous, as well as most infamous characters.

Kevin and his best friend, Dale Shiffman, became ensnarled in the vortex of what is one of baseball's biggest drug scandal – 1985's investigation of the use of cocaine in Major League Baseball. Kevin was offered a deal by the police, he would have to wear a wire and snitch on his best friend in exchange for immunity. Kevin did, and Dale and five other men were convicted of dealing cocaine and sentenced to jail time. Additionally, eleven Pittsburg players received suspensions from the Commissioner of MLB, seven of them for a full season. Dale Shiffman served a 2-year sentence.

Kevin had lost his job with the Pirates, and his fame and fortune along with it. He not only had lost his job with baseball, but he had lost all of his baseball friends. He no longer had any contact with the baseball world he so dearly loved. Likewise, Dale Schiffman's life had changed dramatically. He had not only lost his celebrity lifestyle, he had also lost his freedom. While in prison, Dale became a Christian. When he experienced the forgiveness that Christ offered him, he knew how badly Kevin would need it as well. After serving out his sentence, Dale sought Kevin out to offer him forgiveness for his betrayal. Dale did so, not because Kevin deserved forgiveness, but because Kevin needed his forgiveness. When they finally met, imagine how Kevin would have felt. He had sold out his best friend and sent him to prison to save his own neck. Might he have expected Dale to be angry with him? Probably that or worse. Instead, Dale told Kevin that he had forgiven him for betraying him. Kevin wept uncontrollably. The pain of what he had done to his best friend had been eating at him for years. His own conscious had convicted him to a lifetime of self-torture. Dale gave him the forgiveness he so desperately needed in order to heal. If, and when, we are ready to repent of our sins, and to have faith that God can, and will not only forgive us, but also help us to change, then our lives have begun to be transformed.

...to have God remove...

Paul advises us to allow our lives to be "transformed by the renewing of [our] minds." (Romans 12:2). To be completely honest with ourselves, we must face the truth that we really love some of our defects. For example, pride serves to exalt us above others, to make us feel special when we lack an honest self-esteem based on our identity in Christ. If we surrender our pride, we find we feel less than others, often depressed and insecure. Another example is how being quick to anger, and speaking abusively to others works to protect us from our own feelings of inadequacy, pain or disappointment. Being completely honest in all things requires us to live within the confines of our own limitations, gifts and abilities. Maintaining our relationship with lust sustains an illusion that suppresses our belief that we are alone, unlovable, and unwanted. Step 6 requires us to be ready to give up these and all of our defects of character.

For those of us who have tried to do this on our own, we learned we were powerless to remove these defects of character ourselves. How then, does this change happen? Those who came before us tell us that God could, and would, remove these defects of character, if we became willing to allow Him. Having not had that experience ourselves, we must choose to trust in their wisdom. Choosing to trust in something you cannot see for yourself, but have assurance in, is the definition of Faith (Hebrews 11:1). The vehicle of our journey on the path of recovery is faith.

As we embark on this journey, we have to remember that we should not expect perfection from ourselves, as we often do. We experience these kinds of changes in stops and starts. At times, it is "one step forward and two steps back." However, over time we found that change was indeed happening. In addition, we have to realize that others may be skeptical about our ability to stick to this path and actually change. We have made that promise so many times that we have no stone upon which to stand. Nevertheless, we make this journey for ourselves, not for the approval of others, and often in spite of their derision. The first step on that journey is to confess our wrongs to another person. We learned how to do that when we worked our Fifth Step. The second step is to become willing to allow God to remove our character defects.

...defects of character

When writing about his giving up his own character defect of pride, Paul described the journey this way (Phillippians 3:12-14):

"I don't mean to say that I have already achieved these things or that I have already achieved perfection! But I keep working toward that day when I will finally be all that Christ Jesus saved me for and wants me to be...Forgetting the past and looking forward to what lies ahead, I strain to reach the end of the race and receive the prize for which God, through Christ Jesus, is calling us up to heaven."

Paul admits he is not yet perfect, but he is working towards that perfection.

We may have some fears about letting go of some of our defects. Some of them have been with us for a very long time, while others may be tied to survival skills, or lifestyles. The choice is simple: Surrender our defects to God and choose sobriety, or go back to the insanity of our addiction. Our character defects not only hurt those we offend, they hurt ourselves as well. Wounded by our own actions, we rationalized and defended ourselves, and wound up committing more transgressions. The more we allowed sin to reign in us, the more depraved we became. We have learned where that path goes. That path leads us to insanity and ultimately, death, as sin always does. If we do not die as a direct result of our behaviors, then we die indirectly and eventually. Some of us also died in body as well. The path of recovery offers us the hope of a different path, one that leads back to sanity and to life. The entryway to the path of recovery is repentance.

Willing to be Willing

> *"No action will be considered blameless, unless the will was so, for by the will the act was dictated."*
>
> *— Seneca*

The Sixth step requires us to deal with two things: our will, and our defects. We first have to become willing to allow God to work in us. There are a few things that God cannot do. One of those is to violate our free will. He can only work in us as much as we invite Him to. How, exactly does one become "entirely ready", or "willing" to allow God to do His work? To be "entirely ready" means to be prepared. Imagine yourself getting ready for a trip – you pack your bags, set them by the door, but you don't get dressed! You are not entirely ready! And yet, even when we pack our bags and get dressed, but do not intend to go, we are still not entirely ready, are we? On the one hand, we must "pack our bag" of defects, on the other we must decide to allow God remove them.

As Paul writes to the Christians at Ephesus, we must make one choice to set aside our old sinful ways, and a second choice to put on the "new self" given to us by Christ.

> *"You have been taught…that, in reference to your former manner of life, you lay aside the old self, which is being corrupted in accordance with the lusts of deceit, and that you be renewed in the spirit of your mind, and put on the new self, which in [the likeness of] God has been created in righteousness and holiness of the truth."*
>
> *– Ephesians 4:21-24 (NAS)*

Many of us have wondered how to accomplish this Herculean task. It would indeed be overwhelming if we had to make the "new" self ourselves! The Good News is that Christ has already made a new self for us! The Scriptures frequently uses the image of putting on the new self like one puts on a robe; we do not make the robe, we just put it on. It has been custom-tailored for us by the Creator of all things! We have to choose to give up our "right" to wear our old robe of sinfulness, and choose to wear the cloak of righteousness given to us by Christ.

Many of us objected to this idea, saying that we have tried before, and it did not work. Every time, we went back to our old sinful nature. Yes, we are free to go back to our old, rotten, dirty, stinking clothes whenever we like. That is our choice. But it is not the fault of the robe, and neither it is the fault of the tailor. Our problem is not that God failed us in the past, but that we failed to allow God to help us into the robe.

1) What defects do I have that I like, and may have difficulty letting go of? _____

_____

_____

_____

2) Do I believe that I can change? If no, what prevents me? _____
_____
_____
_____
_____
_____

3) What changes have occurred in me as a result of my recovery work so far? _____
_____
_____
_____
_____
_____

4) What defects do I have that I believe cannot be removed and why? _____
_____
_____
_____
_____
_____

5) How have I attempted to remove my defects on my own? _____
_____
_____
_____
_____
_____

6) How well did my attempts work? _____
_____

7) Do I believe that God can, and will change me if I allow Him? If not, why not? You might want to discuss this with your sponsor and/or accountability partners. _____
_____

8) What do I need to do to be "entirely ready?" _____
_____
_____
_____
_____

9) How does working this step deepen my trust in God? _____
_____
_____
_____
_____

10) What issues of trust and faith do I need to continue to work on with God? _____
_____
_____
_____
_____

Character Surgery

> *"Will is character in action."*
>
> — *William McDougall*

The next thing we must do is to allow God to remove all our character defects. Many of us, reading that phrase, "...have God remove all these defects..." have wondered how that happens. Does God wave His magic wand over our little heads like a fairy godmother turning us from pumpkins to carriages? Well, not exactly. Paul tells us in his letter to the church at Rome how it works:

"Since we have been united with him in his death, we will also be raised as he was. Our old sinful selves were crucified with Christ so that sin might lose its power in our lives. We are no longer slaves to sin. For when we died with Christ we were set free from the power of sin. And since we died with Christ, we know we will also share his new life. We are sure of this because Christ rose from the dead, and he will never die again.

Death no longer has any power over him. He died once to defeat sin, and now he lives for the glory of God. So you should consider yourselves dead to sin and able to live for the glory of God through Christ Jesus. Do not let sin control the way you live; do not give in to its lustful desires. Do not let any part of your body become a tool of wickedness, to be used for sinning. Instead, give yourselves completely to God since you have been given new life. And use your whole body as a tool to do what is right for the glory of God. Sin is no longer your master, for you are no longer subject to the law, which enslaves you to sin. Instead, you are free by God's grace."

— *Romans 6:5-14*

It is vital for us to comprehend what Paul is telling us. He asserts that we are "no longer slaves to sin." He asserts that Christ defeated sin and since Christ lives in us, through His power, we do not have to live a life out of control. The key concept is his point that we should "consider" ourselves dead to sin. To "consider" means to *believe* in this truth. Remember the story about the Great Wallenda and the point about the difference between "believing about" and "believing in"? In this moment, you have to ask yourself if you believe that Christ's work on the cross applies to you or not. If it does, then you have to believe in the fact that you are no longer a slave to sin - you have the ability to choose to not sin.

We have to understand that while "getting it" is an event, like turning on the lightbulb, living a consistently sober life is a process. We have to work within each moment of our lives where a character defects raises its head, to turn it over to God and allow Him to carry it off, and to replace it with His righteousness. With some defects, we have to turn them over again and again. Our experience is that with each letting go, it gets easier and easier.

Every day we have the opportunity to work Step Six. For example, it is in a choice that we have to make to be willing to be completely honest in everything. "Right, but no one is perfect. How can we promise to never tell a lie?" Some argue that it is better to be honest in stages, taking the easier steps first, and working our way up to the harder things. However you approach it, the task is to be "entirely willing," not "entirely perfect." Applying the principle of willingness means that we are willing to act differently. To slip up on an occasion is one thing, but to consciously choose to continue in dishonesty about certain things is an entirely different matter. Unless, and until we are entirely ready to be completely honest, we will continue to be, at our core, dishonest people. And as long as we remain dishonest people, we will not experience growth in our character or our spirits.

Change

"Great souls have wills; feeble ones have only wishes."

— *Chinese Proverb*

In order to change something, we must first identify it and understand its nature. We start by making a list of our character defects, and we take each item on the list and commit it to prayer and conscious effort to allow God to remove it from our lives.

Review your Fourth Step. Make a list of your character defects as you understand them. As a general principle, people don't go "from" something; they go "to" something. Therefore, identify the character asset with which God will replace each of your old character defects. Some samples are provided below:

Defects into Assets

Character Defect .... **Character Asset**

Deceitfulness.. Honesty
Selfishness... Altruism
Self-centeredness .... Other/God-Centeredness
Resentment .... Forgiveness
Fear .... Courage/Trust in God
Pride... Humility
Greed.. Giving/Sharing
Lust .... Worshiping God
Procrastination .... Action
Gluttony .... Moderation
Anger .... Peace
Jealousy... Trust
Impatience... Patience
Criticalness .... Praise
Judgment... Acceptance

Which character defects on your list are most important for you to give up first? For example, if your lack of honesty is leading you to embezzle funds from your employer, that's probably a very important defect to focus on, due to the severe consequences that could arise. Number the items on your list from most important (#1) to least important.

Prayer Journal

If you do not currently maintain a prayer journal, we recommend that you start one with this step. A simple format similar to the one illustrated below is all that is needed. In this exercise you will mark the event of your repentance, and also track your daily process of continuing to allow God to shape your character. In the first entry in the sample prayer journal, you will notice the event of repentance recorded and in the second entry, the continuation of the daily work.

Many of us had to ask, "What, exactly, do we do to repent of something?" We suggest the following ceremony. First, find a quiet place, either alone or with one or two close, supportive believers. Bring the character defect to the Lord in prayer, "Lord, I confess my sin of deceitfulness (or other defect). I acknowledge that I have used dishonesty to control others, to hide my addiction, and to cover my low self-worth. I surrender my right to be dishonest to you. I ask that you fill me with your truth, and that you will help me to be a person of integrity in all things. In Jesus' name, Amen." Repeat as often as needed. That's all there is to it!

On the following page we show you a sample prayer journal. There are many formats for keeping a prayer journal, and this is just one example. The first column is the date of the prayer. The second column records the prayer. The third column is for the result, and the fourth column is for the date the prayer was answered.

Date	Prayer	Result	Date
July 21	Lord, I repent of my deceitfulness.	Told boss I didn't close the deal.	August 1
	Help me to be honest in all things.	He was upset but encouraging.	
August 2	Lord, make me a person of integrity in all things.	Gave excess change back to store clerk.	Aug. 14

Review your list of character defects. Place an asterisk or check mark by each defect that you know will be difficult for you to let go of. For each of them, answer the following questions. Those who have worked this program before us tell us this truth, "When you want to get rid of it more than you want to keep it, you will do so."

1) Why do I want to keep this defect? _____
_____
_____
_____
_____

2) What are the advantages of keeping this defect? _____
_____
_____
_____
_____
_____

3) What are the disadvantages of keeping this defect?_____
_____
_____
_____
_____
_____

4) What are the advantages of letting go of this defect? _____

_____
_____
_____
_____
_____

5) What are the disadvantages of letting go of this defect? _____

_____
_____
_____
_____
_____

6) How strongly do I still want to keep this defect? (0 – 100%, a zero = entirely willing to let go, 100 = determined to keep) _____

7) If I am not yet entirely ready, what do I need to do to become so? Consider discussing this issue with your sponsor to get additional recommendations. _____

_____
_____

According to the 12 Steps & 12 Traditions of Alcoholics Anonymous, "This is the step that separates the men from the boys." Because a person who is capable of being "entirely ready" for God to remove all of his or her defects without reservation is surely entitled to be called "…a [person] who is sincerely trying to grow in the image and likeness of his own Creator."

Congratulations on completing your Sixth Step! Ready for Step Seven?

Step Seven

Humbly asked Him to remove our shortcomings.

"Humility is the modesty of the soul. It is the antidote to pride."

— *Voltaire*

"Hello, my name is Sharon and I am a grateful Christian recovering from sex and love addiction." "Hi Sharon," came the chorus response from the group. "Our program says we should lead with our weaknesses and not with our strengths, so tonight I need to talk about my seventh step…or maybe about how I'm NOT doing my seventh step." A murmur of agreeable chuckles rippled across the room. Sharon continued, "We all know that step seven is where we "*humbly* ask God to remove our shortcomings." My sponsor says that humility is not the absence of pride, but simply the 'reaction of the finite being to the awareness of the presence of the infinite.'" Sharon paused and took a breath. The silence in the room made her acutely aware oh how loudly her heart was beating. Laughing, she said, "Right. I asked her what the heck *that* means…" The group laughed with her… "and **why** the step specifies that we 'humbly' ask. You know? Like what's wrong with 'regular' asking?" The laughter in the room grew even louder.

Humbly...

Humility is the place you arrive at after you have realized that there is a God and that you are not Him, and that you are no better than your fellow man. You might not be humble if you're wondering, "Why do I have to be humble in order for God to remove my shortcomings?" Perhaps it is because unless we recognize the fact that He is God, and we are not, we cannot accept His authority and power. Humility recognizes that we need the help of our Lord and Savior, and that only in humbleness can we truly grant Him an "all access pass" to our hearts and minds.

Steps Four, Five and Six all worked to prepare us for this moment. If we are not aware of our defects, if we have not plumbed the depths of pain they caused others and ourselves, then we cannot possibly be prepared to let them go. Having diligently applied ourselves to the program thus far, we can only be as prepared as we are able, and that will suffice for a beginning. In Step Seven we move in our new and growing faith that God can and will respond to our request to remove our shortcomings.

Step Six taught Bob that he has a significant character defect of dishonesty. He also learned that he has an issue with being prideful. For Bob, his pride and his dishonesty go hand-in-hand. He thinks he shouldn't have to be accountable to anyone about his activities. His pride rebels against the idea of being treated "like a child", in spite of the reality that he has acted far more like a child than an adult. When used in this context, pride is defined as having "…an inordinate opinion of one's own dignity, importance, merit, or superiority, whether as cherished in the mind or as displayed in bearing, conduct, etc."

Pride's synonyms are listed as conceit, vanity and egotism. (Dictionary.com). Just so we are being clear, this is not a good thing to have.

As Voltaire so eloquently penned it, Step Seven offers to Bob the antidote to pride – humility. How does one go about getting humility? Hopefully, having worked the Steps up to this point has brought some humility to you. If pride is the product of having an overly high opinion of yourself, then humility is the product of being acutely aware of your limitations. In his letter to the church at Rome, Paul wrote:

"For by the grace given me I say to every one of you: Do not think of yourself more highly than you ought, but rather think of yourself with sober judgment, in accordance with the measure of faith God has given you."

— *Romans 12:3*

1) How has my understanding of God grown because of my work in the previous Steps?
___
___
___
___
___
___

2) What have I learned about God that leads me to believe that He will remove my shortcomings if I ask Him to? ___
___
___
___
___
___
___

3) What might interfere with my ability to allow God to remove my character defects?
___
___
___
___
___
___

4) Write down two things you can do (e.g., talk to sponsor/pastor) to work on anything that limits your ability to let God do this work. _____

_____
_____
_____
_____
_____

5) How does humility affect my recovery? _____

_____
_____
_____
_____
_____

6) Look up the following verses: Isaiah 57:15, James 4:6 and James 4:10. What is the main point for all of those verses? How does their message relate to the importance of our humility in recovery? _____

_____
_____
_____
_____
_____
_____

...asked Him...

> *"What debilitates our prayer life...is our presupposition that the pressures of life are on one side while God is on some other side."*
>
> *— George MacLeod*

Prayer, on the one hand, is so simple and easy, and on the other impossibly difficult. Why is that? We talk to God, out loud or just in our heads, and that is prayer. While God hears every prayer, it may not be so easy for us to hear Him. There are two things that are in the way of our ability to hear God: 1) fear – the opposite of trust, and 2) pride – the opposite of humility. We have already talked about the importance of humility; but what about fear? For some of us, we still fear God. We still feel so incredibly defective, or bad, that we cannot bear to risk exposing ourselves to Him. We are convinced He could not love or accept us, or worse, that He will be terribly angry with us, and punish us. Sometimes we believe He punishes us whether we talk to Him or not.

We have also learned that some of us fear the vulnerability of openness with God, not because of what He might do, but because of what we might feel. In order to connect with God, to hear God, we must first connect with our own hearts. For most of us, we have worked quite hard at staying away from our feelings and now we have to actually turn and face them? However, the truth is that running away from our feelings by self-medicating with lust was, and is, the problem that caused us to loose so much of our humanity.

1) What is my biggest block to praying openly to God? _____

_____
_____
_____
_____
_____
_____

2) Write down one thing that you will do to learn to be more vulnerable with God. _____

_____
_____
_____
_____
_____
_____
_____

3) Do I need to ask God to remove my shortcomings? Why? _____

_____
_____
_____
_____
_____
_____
_____
_____

4) Read the following verses: Philippians 4:6, Luke 11:13, and Matthew 7:7. What does God's Word have to say about the importance of asking God for what we need? _____

_____
_____
_____
_____
_____
_____
_____
_____
_____
_____

...to remove...

"It was pride that changed angels into devils; it is humility that makes men as angels."

— *Saint Augustine*

When most of us read this step, we wondered when will God remove our defects of character. Does it happen right away, miraculously? Or, does it take a long time? Does it hurt when He takes them out? The answer to all three questions is "Yes...sometimes." Sometimes God removes our defects immediately and miraculously (note, miraculous procedures are typically painless), and sometimes God removes the defects slowly over time (frequently not painless). Sometimes it hurts when we let them go. Whatever the timing of God's work, we can trust that whenever it happens, it happens in His timing, and according to His plan (Jeremiah 29:11).

When Bob finally realized that he was prideful and made the choice to be more accurate in his appraisal of himself he had "surrendered" his pride to Jesus. He worked diligently every day at not being prideful and in the process became acutely aware of how much his pride had, indeed, made him think he was better than other people. He found himself, however, not filled with serenity and peace, but with pain and an achy, hollow feeling. Recognizing that he had begun to think that acting out would be a nice way to cure that ailment, he called his sponsor and invited him out to coffee.

Bob said, "Dwight, I need to understand how this sobriety thing is supposed to help. Right now, I am more miserable now than I was before I got sober! I've lost my wife, my family, my job...acting out is looking like a pretty good idea."

Dwight asked Bob to explain what was going on for him and he listened carefully for several minutes as Bob shared about his letting go of his pride.

Then Dwight answered, "Bob, your relationship with your character defect of pride has helped you, all these years, to feel better than others. Why do you think you needed that?"

"Why do I *need* to feel better than others?" Bob repeated softly. The question hit him like a blow to the chin. He realized the implication immediately, and was shocked to discover how much he resonated with this truth.

After a quiet moment he softly said, "I guess I needed to have a high opinion of myself because inside, I really don't feel all that great about me. My pride, like my addiction, was a way to keep from feeling…I don't know…'less than'?"

"Right" Dwight quietly affirmed. "You have to grieve the loss of your pride, and you also have to deal with your overly low opinion of yourself."

In that moment, as much as Bob was aware of the two pains that he carried within him, he also became aware of a new sense of peace that had begun to grow within him.

Most of us were not prepared for this sense of emptiness that followed the loss of some of our character defects. We have had them for so long, and many of them made us feel special, or important. Without them, we felt empty, small, insignificant, or lost. Someone once lamented that it is indeed, difficult to just walk, like normal people, rather than to fly, as addicts do. In any case, we must learn to re-adjust to life as "normies" and grieve the loss of our defects. At these times, we must work our program even harder, lest we allow ourselves to slide into relapse.

1) Have you ever experienced grief or sadness at the loss of a favored defect? If yes, what was the defect and how did letting go of it change you? _____

_____
_____
_____
_____
_____

2) Write down three healthy things you can do to cope with your feelings about the loss of one or more of your character defects:

a) _____

_____
_____
_____

b) _____

_____
_____
_____

c) _____

3) What do the following verses have to say about HOW God will replace my defects? John 14:26, Galatians 5:16, Ephesians 3:16 _____

...our shortcomings.

> "Without humility there can be no humanity."
>
> — *John Buchan*

Our "shortcomings" are our character defects, those attitudes and perceptions that cause us to act as if we were the only person in the world. After all, it is all about us, isn't it? Some examples of character defects are ego, pride, self-centeredness, selfishness, impatience, jealousy, and willfulness. In our program, we have learned to replace character defects with spiritual principles. Where we have been self-centered, we must learn to serve others. Where in the past we would have insisted on our own timing, we must learn to practice patience. We must learn to replace pride with humility. Additionally we must learn to replace willfulness with surrender, jealousy with trust, and self-pity with faith.

1) Have I accepted powerlessness over my shortcomings, as well as my addiction? If not, how do I plan to help myself accept my powerlessness? _____

2) How does working this step challenge and deepen my trust in Jesus? _____

3) How do we know if God is replacing our character defects? What is the significance of the following verse in light of this question? Galatians 5:22 – 23 _____

_____

_____

_____

Take each of the following spiritual principles and give a recent example of a time when you had opportunity to practice that principle and failed.

Serving Others: _____

_____

_____

Patience: _____

_____

_____

Humility: _____

_____

_____

Surrender: _____

_____

_____

Trust: _____

_____

_____

Faith: _____

_____

_____

Now take each of the spiritual principles and give an example of a time when you had an opportunity to practice that principle and succeeded.

Serving Others: _____

_____

_____

_____

Patience: _____

_____

_____

_____

Humility: _____

_____

_____

_____

Surrender: _____

_____

_____

_____

Trust: _____

_____

_____

_____

Faith: _____

_____

_____

_____

For each spiritual principle listed, write about how you can work on practicing that principle this week. How will Jesus help you develop that spiritual principle? Find a verse that instructs you on that spiritual principle.

Serving Others: _____

_____

_____

Verse: _____

Patience: _____
_____
_____

Verse: _____
_____

Humility:_____
_____
_____

Verse: _____
_____

Surrender: _____
_____
_____

Verse: _____

Trust:_____
_____
_____

Verse: _____

Faith:_____
_____

Prayer Journal

    The last component to working this step is to track God's work in your character re-development. In Step 6 we laid out the structure for a basic prayer journal. If you didn't start one then, now is the time to catch up. All you need is a small notepad, and a pencil or pen. You'll make three columns, as shown in the following example. Character changes often happen in small increments and quiet moments. As such, they are easily forgotten. This prayer journal tool is quite effective at helping us remember the changes and watch the progress of God's work in our hearts and minds. For each character defect, write down the defect, the date you asked God to remove the defect, the prayer request itself, and document the changes as they happen.

Date	Defect	Prayer: Changes & Date
10/2/06	Pride	Lord, I turn my pride over to you.
		10/5: beginning to realize that I'm just the same as everyone else.
		Replace it with your humility.
11/21/06	Impatience	Jesus, I surrender my impatience. Replace it with your Grace.
		11/22: Wow! I see how my impatience is related to my pride. I can wait for others as long as I don't see myself as more important than them!

The Seventh Step, as all of the others, is one that we work at every day, and will do so for the rest of our lives. Some of our character defects leave us quickly, and others require our regular attention. We are, after all, still just as human as everyone else on the planet is, and not yet perfect. Lord, help us to accept your offer to shine through us, that where we are weak, you are strong, and that the end product not be us, but you living through us more clearly than ever before.

Step Eight

Made a list of all persons we had harmed, and became willing to make amends to them all.

> "Never can true courage dwell with them, who, playing tricks with conscience, dare not look at their own vices."
>
> — Samuel Taylor Coleridge

Bob had barely finished his seventh step when he began to think about the daunting task of the next step that awaited him. Steps Eight and Nine caused his stomach to churn from the very first time he read through the Twelve Steps. The list of persons he had harmed was going to be very, very long. Bob decided to just tell his sponsor about the struggle he was having.

"I can't do Step Eight, Dwight" Bob confessed.

"What do you mean you "can't" do Step Eight?" asked Dwight.

"I mean that every time I think about doing it my stomach knots up and I just can't do it!" Bob complained.

"Ok," said Dwight. "What is it about doing step eight that has you so upset?"

"I don't think I can face all of those people, Dwight. I think I've hurt a lot of people. They're gonna be really mad at me if I try and make amends."

Dwight said, "Bob, you don't actually have to tell anybody anything during Step Eight. That doesn't happen until Step Nine, IF then. Let's just focus on Step Eight and we'll deal with Step Nine when we get there. Ok?"

As the insight melted the stress off his face, Bob just stared at Dwight for a moment. "Sshheessh...you're right. I guess that's why you're the sponsor, huh."

Dwight chuckled lightly and replied, "Yea, I guess we sponsors are good for something, aren't we?"

A moment later, Bob started in again, "Yea, but still, when I get to step nine, I'll have to deal with that!"

Firmly, Dwight replied, "Stop futurizing, Bob. Remember our principles of 'one step at a time, one moment at a time' and 'first things first'?"

"Yea," answered Bob. "Ok then," said Dwight. "Stick to the program."

Step Eight is a step of preparation. The efforts we put into Step Eight are designed to make us ready for the harder work that is to follow in Step Nine. If we do not adequately prepare ourselves, we will fail miserably in our efforts at our Ninth Step. Many of us read this step and thought, "Piece of cake! "Finally, a short step!" Perhaps we are in a hurry to "finish" our step work. Would we be addicts if we weren't compulsive about stuff? Unfortunately, the Eighth Step cannot be done quickly, or without careful consideration.

You've heard the old saying that you can lead a horse to water but you can't make him drink? Well, that's not exactly true; you can, if you make the horse thirsty before you take him to the trough. By working Step Eight, we are making ourselves "thirsty" for the water that we hope for in Step Nine. That "water" is forgiveness, reconciliation, and restoration. As addicts, we have lived our lives as separate from others. In some ways, that separateness made us feel special, or maybe even better than others, but in other ways, it reinforces our secret belief that we are somehow defective, or less than others. These two steps are key assisting us in our task of rejoining the human race.

In Step Nine, we will offer amends to some or all of the people we have harmed in the past. Not only must we be prepared to admit our responsibility in a sincere and helpful fashion, we must be prepared to receive the reaction of those we have wounded. Think briefly about those persons on your amends list; are there any potential reactions that create fear or anxiousness for you? Are there people from your past you have been avoiding? In order to accomplish Steps Eight and Nine, we have to develop the character asset of courage.

Courage does not arrive like a package underneath our Christmas tree with a bow on top, waiting for us to unwrap it and play with it like a new toy. It can only be found by choosing to walk down the dark and frightening path of our own past. Courage is not an emotion. No one ever feels courageous. Courage is the act of choosing to do something in spite of our fears. In the insanity of our addiction, we caused damage to many others, and Steps Eight and Nine require us to inventory the damage we did to those persons, and to make our amends in spite of our worry about how they will react.

Responsibility, Repentance, & Commitment

"Repentance, of all things in the world, makes the greatest change; it changes things in heaven and earth; for it changes the whole man from sin to grace."

— *Jeremy Taylor*

Once we understood what awaited us, most of us asked one or more of the following types of questions: "Do I really have to do this? What is the point? How will it help to stir up all that old history? Shouldn't we just let 'sleeping dogs lie'?" The answer to the first question is "Yes" (you weren't really expecting to see "No" here, were you?). To answer the other questions we have to consider the impact on us of working these steps. Our addiction has damaged our relationship with the world in which we live in so many ways, and Steps Eight and Nine help to restore our "rightness" with the world. As our sponsors have told us, "sleeping dogs don't lie, they lay in wait." In other words, if we don't repair the damages we have done, they won't repair themselves; they only wait for the path of your life to carry you nearby, and then they jump up out of the ground and bite you on the behind. We can never truly move ahead while we are anchored to our past through our denials, rationalizations and entitlements. Making our amends severs those ties and allows us to grow and mature, and restores our "right standing" with the world.

Our program teaches us that there are two important aspects to Step Eight: We must take responsibility for our past behaviors, and we must repent from our sins.

Responsibility

"Does anyone really believe he can escape from the responsibility for what he has done and thought in secret?...The centre of our whole being is involved in the centre of all being; and the centre of all being rests in the centre of our being."

— Paul Tillich

We began taking responsibility for our sins the moment we admitted to ourselves that we had a problem. We have continued that process of accepting personal responsibility through each of the previous steps. Responsibility exists in many different levels. We can take responsibility internally, by acknowledging to ourselves that this fact or that thing is true about us. We can also take responsibility externally, by acknowledging to others that we own this event or that behavior. Finally, we can take direct responsibility by acknowledging to the person or persons we harmed that we are aware that we caused them harm.

In our Fourth Step, we made a list of resentments, and the people, places, and things that were connected to our resentments. Many of us found it helpful to review that list for candidates for our Eighth Step. Bear in mind there may be people who need to be on our Eighth Step list who are not on our Fourth Step list.

Many of us also found that there were people from our life whom we were reluctant to put on this list. Some of that desire to avoid comes from our own fear of having to talk to that person in our Ninth Step (potentially). For some of us, the issue is an unresolved resentment with that person. In that case, we are still more concerned with what that person did to us, than we are with what we did to them. Perhaps we even justified our actions based upon what they did to us. We need to revisit our Fourth Step work on that person.

Consider the following verses and their implications for the importance of forgiveness in our lives and others' lives. Look up these verses and write them in the space provided:

Colossians 3:13 _____
_____
_____
_____

Ephesians 4:32 _____
_____
_____
_____

Mark 11:25 _____
_____

Matthew 6:14-15 _____

1) How does a lack of forgiveness impact our relationship with God? _____

2) Do you know anyone who has an obvious lack of forgiveness towards others? If yes, how would you describe them? How does their lack of forgiveness impact them? _____

3) What lack of forgiveness do you have and how does it impact you? _____

4) Ask someone who knows you well, if they have observed any unforgiveness in you and if so, to describe how that impacts how they see you. _____

5) If you are not ready to deal with that person at this time, write down an action plan for how you will help yourself to become willing to address that issue. _____

_____
_____
_____
_____

Repentance

> *"Repentance is not self-regarding, but God-regarding. It is not self-loathing, but God-loving."*
>
> — *Fulton J. Sheen*

One of the most important parts of being "willing" in Step Eight is to prepare ourselves by repenting of all of the sins we have inventoried. In the New Testament, the Greek word for repentance (μετανοια) is translated as, "metanoia", or to change one's mind (literally, a change of knowing). If we have not repented, or changed our minds about our past behaviors, our efforts at making amends in Step Nine will prove fruitless. After all, what good would an amends to someone be, if we continue doing the same things that caused us to injure them in the first place?

Repentance is often accompanied by a feeling of remorse or regret, whose appearance is logical since the change of mind involves the recognition that the previous opinion was false or bad. For example, when we engage in our acting out behaviors we are operating under a belief that what we are doing is OK or justifiable. After all, if we really believed the thing was wrong, we would not do it.

Many have protested that they have "repented" so many times in the past and it never made any difference. So, what then, is the problem? Most of us learned that it was not so much the repentance itself that failed us. We looked back on an event and saw that it was bad, and felt sorrowful, and swore off that behavior. However, eventually we found ourselves back in the same position.

The wisdom of those who went before us is that what failed was not our repentance, but our ability to remember our new opinion that the thing was bad to do. We somehow forgot to remember it. Therefore, we allowed our mind to revert to what we believed previously.

There is an often-repeated story about the founder of Alcoholics Anonymous, Bill Wilson that highlights this principle. The story goes that Bill was called by a physician friend of his to come talk to a fellow at the hospital, who the doctor said would die very soon if he did not stop drinking. Bill obliged his friend and paid a call to the man in his hospital room. Bill introduced himself, and promptly received a thorough tongue-lashing from the man, who apparently felt insulted that someone thought he had a drinking problem. In short, the man told Bill he didn't need his help or saving, and to take his hypocrisy elsewhere. Bill responded forthrightly that he was not there to save him, but that he was there to save himself. Bill explained, every time he sees someone like him, it helps him to remember where he will wind up if he goes back to drinking. That way, he does not forget. Still today, I hear people in meetings say that the newcomer is the most important person in the meeting, because it reminds us of where we came from, and where we do not want to return. Working Steps Eight and Nine are often helpful for many of us in knowing and remembering, so that we do not forget.

In Step Six we applied the spiritual principle of repentance to our character defects. In Step Eight we will apply it to our past behaviors, and specifically to those behaviors that injured others. Go back through your Moral Inventory list from Step Four and create a list of behaviors from which you need to repent. Do you remember our important principle in recovery: That we will continue in our old ways until we get new ways to replace them? For each behavior that we have to repent from, we have to commit ourselves to a new behavior that we will choose instead of the old one.

Commitment

> *"Unless you can find some sort of loyalty, you cannot find unity and peace in your active living."*
>
> *— Josiah Royce*

Repentance without commitment is like a guitar without strings. The guitar can be made of the most beautiful woods and masterly handcrafted, but without strings, it cannot fulfill its purpose of making beautiful music. When we change our way of thinking about the behavior without having an associated commitment to keep our mind changed about the behavior, we will all too quickly change our minds back.

One of the most difficult things to do in recovery is to keep our commitment to staying sober: Getting sober is easy, staying sober is not. The wisdom of our program gives us several tips on how to keep our sobriety. First, we must remind ourselves every day of our new perspective on our old behaviors. You may have heard the saying that we keep our sobriety, "one day at a time, each moment at a time." Part of the wisdom of this saying is that we have to remind ourselves, as often as needed, sometimes moment to moment, that our old life was bankrupt and that staying sober is the only way to have any peace in our life. The second tip our program provides for us is that the only way to keep our sobriety is to give it away. Amazingly, when we give back to program, whether by setting up chairs before a meeting or by being available as an accountability partner, we find an additional level of awareness of the importance of our sobriety. Another tip that our program gives us is our recovery chips. That little piece of plastic attached to our keychain serves as a physical and gentle reminder all day of our connection to recovery.

A great tool to help work on commitment is to take your completed Repentance Worksheet (see the following exercise) and transfer it to a 3 X 5 card to keep in your hip pocket. You write the Old Behavior and Old Belief on the front of the card, and then the New Belief, Repentance, and New Behavior on the back of the card. Whenever you need, you can review it to refresh whatever part of your memory is failing you at the time.

The Repentance Worksheet

This particular project can take quite a long time to work through adequately, so take your time. Remember we are in no hurry to finish anything, as we are on a journey that can only be fully enjoyed at a walking pace. Occasionally, we even need to stop and smell the roses. Many of us have had difficulty in identifying our old beliefs, or in creating new beliefs with which to replace them. Rather than allowing our frustration to cause us to stop our efforts, we found that turning to our sponsors and accountability partners for feedback often helped us gain the insight and understanding we needed to continue our journey. Some of us needed the additional assistance of a pastor, professional counselor or therapist.

The Repentance Worksheet is a tool that we use to help us sort out what we have to repent from and what "change of mind" we need to have. It is a five column technique where we identify: 1) the old problem behavior, 2) the belief(s) we had at that time that enabled us to do that thing, 3) our new belief about that behavior, 4) what our repentance should be, and 5) what new behaviors we are going to choose instead of the old ones. While the Worksheet is simple, the task of filling it out is not. Make sure to stay in close contact with your sponsor and accountability partners while you hammer out these details. Ask for feedback or assistance whenever needed, and bathe the task in prayer frequently.

On the following page we present a sample Repentance Worksheet. A section of Bob's Repentance Worksheet illustrates how we work from our old behaviors to create new beliefs and behaviors.

REPENTANCE WORKSHEET

Old Behavior	Old Belief	New Belief	Repentance	New Behavior
Leaving early from work to go act out.	I work hard and deserve the treat.	When I leave early I steal time from my employer	Lord, I acknowledge it is wrong to take what is not mine. I surrender my right to do so and choose honesty and integrity.	Set up accountability for leaving on time.
Telling my wife I am working late when I am really going to the strip club.	It doesn't really matter if I come home a little later tonight.	Lying to my wife damages her trust as well as our intimacy.	Jesus, I know dishonesty hurts my wife, my self-esteem, and my ability to be close to you. I will choose intimacy with you, with her, and personal integrity.	Use accountability partners and sponsor to confess when I am tempted to lie.

Made a list of all persons we had harmed...

Ready? Ok, go ahead...make a list of ALL the people you have harmed in your life.

Are you finished yet? Not so easy, is it? Ok, seriously, take the time you need to make your list. Whom do you include on this list? Everyone you have ever harmed. Here are some possibilities: friends, ex-friends, wives, ex-wives, bosses, former bosses, siblings, step-siblings, half-siblings, parents, step-parents, ex-step-parents, neighbors, former neighbors, cousins, second cousins, strangers, one-night-standers, co-workers, sales people, pastors, teachers, and baby sitters. When you have finished the list, let it rest for a few days and then come back and reread it. Make any revisions you find necessary at that time. Then, come back to the next section in this guide.

...and became willing...

This phrase causes many of us to wonder what it means to "become willing." From one perspective, it is a choice, an act of the will. It means to surrender our will to the will of God. It is not the act of doing the thing; it is simply choosing to be obedient to God's direction. Another perspective on becoming "willing" requires us to understand what it is that makes us "unwilling". Once we understand the attitudes, beliefs, and emotions that cause us to balk at the task, we can work at transforming them into attitudes and beliefs that will result in the birth of our willingness.

1) What is it that is important to you about not doing this step? _____

_____
_____
_____
_____

2) What emotions are you most aware of when you think about doing this step? (e.g., guilt, shame, sadness, grief, anger, embarrassment, fear, or anxiety) _____

_____
_____
_____
_____

3) What attitudes or beliefs do you have that are creating these strong emotions? (e.g., even having a new perspective that certain things you did in your past are wrong can generate a strong emotion such as embarrassment.) _____

_____
_____
_____
_____

4) What are the top five advantages to you of not doing this step? _____

_____
_____
_____
_____
_____

5) What are the top five advantages to you of completing this step? _____

_____
_____
_____
_____
_____

Are you ready? Or, at least are you willing to be willing? If not, talk with your sponsor about what is in your way. Otherwise, let's move on!

...to make amends...

Make a what? Most of us never heard the word "amends" until we came to program. Even then, we had to look it up in the dictionary:

AMENDS –

> 1: to put right; especially : to make emendations in (as a text)
> 2: to change or modify for the better ; IMPROVE <amend the situation>
> intransitive senses : to reform oneself
>
> — *Merriam-Webster Dictionary*

Those who have gone before us in recovery have discovered three principles to making an amends: Resolution, Restoration, and Restitution. Resolution simply refers to our "re – solution" or finding an answer to the problem that has been bothering or disturbing us in some way. Our guilty conscience has been knocking on our door for a long time and making an amends can return a portion of our own peace and serenity. Restoration means to return whatever we have damaged to its original condition. In relationship terms, we might have to restore a trust that was broken, or a reputation that was damaged. Restitution refers to compensating someone, monetarily or in equivalency, for his or her losses.

Making amends, it turns out, is not a new idea. In the Old Testament (Leviticus 6:1-7), the Law of Moses specifies that to make an amends for stealing, the individual is to return the stolen amount plus an additional 20% to the victim. In addition, the person also had to take an offering to the priest. As Christians, we are no longer under Old Testament law, or this part of recovery might be complicated! We are, fortunately, under the grace and forgiveness afforded us by Christ.

The majority of our "amends making" involves the confession of our wrongdoing to those we harmed, and asking for their forgiveness. In doing so, our attempt is to modify the damaged relationship for the better, and to restore our standing with our fellow man (or woman, as the case may be). By these actions, we hope for healing not only for ourselves, but for those we harmed. As the principle is to "modify for the better," we do not make amends where to do so would actually make things worse (see Step Nine).

How do we actually make amends? We make amends according to the nature of the damage we have done. Where we have damaged property, we look to offer restitution to the property owner. This is likely the easiest type of amends to make; we get an estimate of the cost of the damage and we replace what was damaged or we provide payment for it. We do recommend that where property damage is involved that the Old Testament principal of adding 20% to the payment is a good rule of thumb to follow. Consider the extra payment remuneration for the inconvenience the property owner has suffered. Damaged relationships, however, are much more challenging to amend: We cannot control the responses of our amendees nor whether they will accept our amends or not. Nonetheless, we attempt to reconcile and restore the relationship wherever possible. We will talk more specifically in Step Nine about the different ways we can attempt to amend a damaged relationship.

...to them all

Everyone? Yes, everyone.

Take the list that you made earlier in this step of all the people you have harmed and read it through thoughtfully. If you don't have paper and pen handy, go get it: We'll wait for you.

Are you back so soon? Seriously, go re-read your list.

Now, are you truly ready? Ok, let's get going.

We use the Amends Preparation Worksheet to help us plan our amends. We start by identifying the person(s) involved and what happened. Then we identify the harm that we caused and the impact of the event upon us. Earlier we talked about the fact that repentance involves a change of mind or belief about the thing that we did. Therefore, next we identify what our new belief is. Finally, we identify the type of amends that we have to make.

We will address the types of amends to make in more detail when we get to Step Nine. For now, the major categories are: Direct, Indirect, and Partial. The subtypes are: Restitution, Restoration, and Apology. In some situations, for example, you may need to do a Direct Apology or Direct Restitution, and in other situations, you may need to do an Indirect Restoration. You will come back to this worksheet in Step Nine and may need to adjust the details at that time. Do not obsess too much on the labels at this point.

This worksheet serves as a rough blueprint for helping us to think about what we did and what we need to do about it. The next step will be to write out a draft of the specific amends in as much detail as possible. For example, if we need to make an apology, we should write out our apology first, review it with our sponsor and accountability partners, and make appropriate edits prior to offering the amends.

As we work through this exercise, we will discover if we have any unwillingness to be willing. We take what we discover to our sponsors, accountability partners, counselors and pastors, and ask for input and direction in how to deal with our unwillingness.

The following page shows a portion of Sharon's list to serve as an example of how to make your own.

Amends Preparation Worksheet

Person(s)	What Happened	Harm I Caused	Impact Upon Me	New Belief	Type of Amends Needed
Bruce	We used porn in our marriage.	1) Made both of us into sexual objects.	1) Damaged my self-esteem	1) Sex is not the same thing as, nor a substitute for intimacy.	Direct
		2) Lusted after someone other than my husband.	2) Emotions: shame, remorse, embarrassment, grief, anxiety & depression.		
			3) Reinforced my belief that my body is inadequate, and that my sexuality should be like the women in porn.	2) I am forgiven by God, & I hope to be forgiven by Bruce.	
Tom	I had an affair with him.	1) Betrayed the trust of my spouse.	1) Emotions: shame, remores, grief.	1) Sex outside of marriage is damaging in many ways.	Direct
		2) Broke my promise to him, God, & myself.	2) Reinforced my belief that I am defective.	2) Trust & respect are more important than sex.	
Jane	I had affair with her husband, Tom.	1) Betrayed the trust of my friend.	1) Emotions: shame, remores, grief.	1) Friendship is more important than sex.	Direct
			2) Reinforced my belief that I am defective.	2) I am wounded, not defective.	
Geoff	1) Took paid time to go rendezvous.	1) I didn't give the company the work they paid for.	1) Emotions: Shame	1) Work time is not mine to take and spend as I please.	Direct
			2) Damaged my integrity.		
	2) Used company computer for personal activities.	2) Betrayed my boss' trust.	3) Cost me manager's respect.	My time is bought by my employer.	

Now that your worksheet is complete, you are finished with your work on Step Eight. Our work in Step Eight has helped us to begin to take responsibility for our behaviors and their consequences. Additionally, we have taken an honest inventory of these behaviors and repented of the attitudes and beliefs that made it possible for us to indulge them. We hope that you are now prepared to take the critically important, and sometimes difficult, actions that will be asked of us in Step Nine. In Step Nine we will discuss the different types of amends and the specifics of constructing your amends. You will make a draft of each amends you need to offer and review it with your accountability partners, sponsors, pastors, counselors and therapists. For now, take a deep breath and give yourself a break. You have worked hard. Remember to keep your life in balance.

Step Nine

Made direct amends to such people wherever possible, except when to do so would injure them or others.

> "Humanity is never so beautiful as when praying for forgiveness, or else forgiving another."
>
> — Jean Paul Richter

The morning arrived like every other morning Bob had ever experienced – with the sun rising just as bright as ever. However, it seemed to Bob that a cloud hung low over his head. After brushing his teeth, he stared at himself in the mirror. "Are you really going to do this thing?" he asked himself. Another long moment's stare and he replied to his reflection, "What doesn't kill you makes you stronger, right?" Bob quickly turned and made his way through his bedroom, down the hallway, and slid behind the wheel of his car inside of his garage. In a matter of minutes, he would be sitting face-to-face with one of his amendees. This would be his first amends, and to say that he was nervous would be an understatement. He'd just as soon have his head put in a vise than to go and have the conversation he was about to attempt. He muttered a quick prayer, "Lord, please give me the courage I need to see this through." Opening the garage door, he threw the car in reverse, backed down his driveway into the street, stopped, and then pointed the front end towards the east side of town.

Step Nine is a step of action. Some have called Step Nine the "path of humility." In this step, more so than any other, we must humble ourselves and face the consequences of our wrongdoing. Most of the work we have done to this point has been to prepare us to take the action(s) required in Step Nine. Here we offer amends to people we have harmed in the past. Remember, we would not be prepared to offer amends without the spiritual growth afforded us by our preceding step work.

Made direct amends...

We have learned that the best amends is a direct amends. A direct amends means, in most cases, a face-to-face meeting. When we are direct and brief, we come across as taking full responsibility for our behavior. When we stroll around the outfield, we may find ourselves alone in the park. We have also learned to be careful to take responsibility for our wrong attitudes, which led to the behavior, and not to offer explanations, as those often sound to others as if we do not really think we were wrong in the first place. There may be situations where a direct amends is not possible, but these should be the exceptions to the rule, and taken under advisement with sponsors first. Our sponsors will help us examine our motives for telling people about our addiction.

While the preferred method of amends-making is direct, there may be situations where we are unable to make the amends face-to-face; for example, in a situation where the person has passed on, or has moved beyond our ability to locate him or her. In these situations, we may make an indirect amends. Some examples of indirect amends include making restitution to our amendee's survivors, or to a favorite charity in their name. We may also write letters that we never send, and pray for those we know are still living but cannot locate. Finally, the best indirect amends we can offer to everyone is to live our lives as changed people, having learned from our mistakes.

There could be other situations where only a partial amends is possible, or advisable. In these situations, a full amends is deemed likely to injure our amendee or others. We must be careful to examine our motivations to offer a partial amends, to ensure that we are not seeking to avoid dealing with the consequences of our sins. A partial amends is properly motivated only by a careful consideration for others. Examples include where we have had an extramarital relationship, and to make a full amends would expose the person with whom we had the affair, resulting in damage to him or her and their families. Or perhaps to even make a full amends to our own spouse, which is highly likely to be damaging to him or her, is a situation which has to be approached very carefully, and may require us to make only a partial amends.

A note about written amends: We should avoid giving our amendees written amends for several reasons. The first reason is that difficulties with communicating very sensitive and personal information in written format are numerous, and include wrong interpretations, and the inability to clarify and respond in a timely fashion. Secondly, they provide an all-too concrete reminder of the very offenses we are trying to move beyond. If we leave a written record of the offense, it serves to keep the offense fresh in the reader's mind. We want our amends to replace the memory of the offense. The third reason is that some people assert that our written amends amounts may be considered a legal document, usable in a court of law. We are to avoid making amends when to do so would injure them or others, and "others" includes our families. Finally, a written amends lacks the fullness of the assumption of personal responsibility that we are seeking to grow, as it helps us avoid relating directly to the person and their reactions to our amends. We cannot truly develop courage by taking half-measures.

Bob sat in his car in the parking lot, his hands tightly gripping the steering wheel. He glanced at his wristwatch and confirmed, once again, that the moment had arrived. He wiped the moisture from his palms on his jeans, took a deep breath, and exited his vehicle. Entering the small, family restaurant, his eyes took in the tables, anxiously scanning for his amendee. "Not here, hmmm." Bob thought.

The cheerful voice of the hostess intruded upon his thoughts, "How many?" she asked.

"Ahhh...I'll need a table for two, someplace quiet, please." Bob replied.

Amends vs. Apologies

It is important that we understand the difference between an amends and an apology. An apology is an expression of regret for having injured another. An amends means to actually change the situation for the better. In recovery, an apology is not considered an adequate amends, although an adequate amends may include an apology.

Consider the following example from the Gospel According to Luke:

"When he came to his senses, he said, 'How many of my father's hired men have food to spare, and here I am starving to death! I will set out and go back to my father and say to him: Father, I have sinned against heaven and against you. I am no longer worthy to be called your son; make me like one of your hired men.'"

— Luke 15:17-19

Is this a good example of amends-making? If yes, why? _____

_____
_____
_____
_____
_____
_____
_____
_____

Did you notice that the son prepared his amends in advance? He carefully thought through what his sins were and what he would say to his father. He was brief and direct about it. More importantly, he changed his attitudes and behaviors, which make this not just an apology, but also an amends.

"May I fill your glass again, sir?" asked the waitress.

Bob checked his watch and replied, "Sure, one more time I guess. Thanks."

Just as the waitress turned to walk away, Bob noticed the door to the restaurant swing open and saw a tall, brunette woman walk brusquely in. She hesitated a moment when she caught his eye, then resolutely lowering her chin, she headed toward his table.

Standing, Bob greeted her, hand extended, "Hi Mary, its good to see you."

Respect

"The more things a man is ashamed of, the more respectable he is."

— George Bernard Shaw

The primary principle we have learned to apply when working our ninth step is respect – for ourselves and for the people to whom we seek to make amends. Of all the steps we have worked thus far, none should be approached with more caution and care than Step Nine. We must not quickly jot down our Step Eight list, and then rush right out and start making amends. Working the Ninth Step may take months, even years, or perhaps never, be complete. We have learned to demonstrate respect for our own processes while working this step, as well as for the potential impact of our amends upon our amendee. We must be prepared for the possibility that some people may not be interested in even speaking to us, much less in receiving an amends from us.

...wherever possible...

That phrase, "wherever possible," is a very important concept in working our Ninth Step. As addicts, it is often difficult for us to understand and accept boundaries and limitations. Many times, we bulldoze our way into or through situations without remembering to respect other's rights and wishes. We need to practice the principle of patience, especially in the working of our program. God has a plan for all things, including the possibility and timing of our making a specific amends. He has an appointed time and place for us to make our amends, and we should be patient and wait for it, not force it. When it is possible, it proceeds, and when it is not possible, we must gracefully walk away. We also need to accept that we may not be able to make certain amends, ever.

"Waitress! Could you bring my friend an iced tea, please?" Bob inquired.
"'Friend'? That's what I am to you?" accused Mary as she glared at him across the table.
"Ahh, right" said Bob. "I guess that would be overstating the case?"
"What's the point, Bob? Why are we doing this?" stated Mary.
"Well, I'm...ahh...that is, I...I need to...or rather I would like to...if its ok with you...to make an amends with you." He managed to stammer out.
"An amends? You in some kind of rehab program or something?" asked Mary.
"Yea, sorta." Said Bob. "I'm trying to...make things right, I guess."
"Well, are you or aren't you?" she said.
"Aren't I what?" said Bob.
"Are you or are you not trying to make things right?" she replied.
"Oh, yes, I am, definitely...am." He replied.
"Go ahead" she deadpanned.
Taking a deep and audible breath, Bob said, "Ok, well...I've been doing a lot of thinking and I've realized how many mistakes I've made in my life...how I haven't always done the 'right' thing with some people...with you, for example."

"Really" she said. "I was a 'mistake'?"

"No! No, that's not what I mean. You weren't a mistake, you were a... a great thing! You were the best thing to happen to me. I made a mistake in leaving you." Bob said.

"Really? Mary asked. "I was a 'great thing...the best thing to happen to you'? Then what's my favorite band?"

"Your favorite band?" parroted Bob.

"Too hard for you? How about my favorite color? Or my favorite desert? Oh, I know an easy one, Bob. How about my middle name?"

"Aaahhh..." Bob said, leaving his jaw hanging open slightly.

"Got nothing?" said Mary.

"Right." said Bob. "Look, I get it. I'm a liar. I don't really know even the simplest of things about you. Things I *should* know if I really cared about you...or anyone."

"Wow. 'Honesty.' Is that insight I smell as well? Seriously Bob, am I supposed to be impressed now or something?" challenged Mary.

"You are really, really angry with me, Mary. I can't say that I blame you. I treated you badly."

"YOU wooed me, YOU wined me and dined me, YOU made me fall for you, YOU laid me, and then YOU LEFT ME!" blurted Mary.

Bob, looked nervously around at the other customers staring at them, and then forced himself to meet Mary's glaring gaze. He smiled weakly and replied in a soft voice, "You're right. I used you. I treated you like a challenge, like a mountain to be climbed or something. I wasn't really in love with you, I was too in love with myself. I..."

"You bastard!" Mary spit her words at him like they were poisioned arrows.

Bob flinched involuntarily and paused a moment while he took a deep breath. "Yes, you are exactly right." Bob agreed. "I was a selfish, self-centered, self-absorbed, ego maniac and I used you. I understand that now. I am so sorry, Mary. You didn't deserve to be treated that way. I am hoping to find some way to ask for your forgiveness, even though I don't deserve it."

They sat there and allowed the silence to grow between them, both trying to figure out what to say next.

"Need any more tea?" asked the overly cheerful waitress who had just appeared at their table.

...*except when to do so would injure them or others.*

> *"If the other person injures you, you may forget the injury;*
> *but if you injure him you will always remember."*
>
> *— Kahlil Gibran*

How do we decide whether our attempt to make an amends will result in an injury to them or someone else? We have learned that the principles of seeking wise counsel and the Lord's guidance are the best ways to decide whether or not to make the amends. We seek the wisdom of those who have gone before us in recovery, our sponsors and other mentors in the program; and we seek the guidance of our Lord through prayer and meditation.

Take a moment to re-read the story of Bob's amends with Mary. What do you notice about how he approached her and how he responded to her? Do you think Bob did an adequate job of thinking through his approach and Mary's reactions? Did he think through whether his amends would cause her harm or not? Should he not have approached her at all? Or, perhaps done so in some other fashion? Later on, you get to read the rest of their conversation and we will re-visit this idea. In all likelihood he did, but this is a good example of how unpredictable people can be. A couple of important points to highlight are Bob's reactions to Mary's anger and attacks at him. First, he maintained a "non-defensive" mental stance. That is to say that he did not attempt to defend himself against her labels or accusations against him. He didn't try and explain them or argue with her about anything. Secondly, Bob used a simple tool for defusing any "critics" in you life. If you want to defeat a critic, simply agree with them. If they say you are the lousiest excuse for a human being, just say, "You are probably right, I might be the worst person ever to walk the planet." When you agree with the critic you take the wind out of their sails and they'll have nothing to say. If you argue with them, or defend yourself, they will simply criticize you more. Try it sometime, it is an amazing tool!

Review your list of the persons you believe you owe an amends to (from Step 8), and answer the following questions of each:

1) Do they know already? _____

_____

_____

_____

_____

_____

2) If not, do they need to know and why? _____

_____

_____

_____

_____

_____

3) What good purpose will be served by sharing such information? _____

_____

_____

_____

_____

_____

4) What damage could such information do? _____

_____
_____
_____
_____
_____

5) What type of amends do I need to make and why? (Direct, Indirect, or Partial)

_____
_____
_____
_____
_____

6) If making other than a direct amends, what are my motives?

_____
_____
_____
_____
_____

7) What will my amends be? For example if my amends will be verbal, what, exactly, will I say?

_____
_____
_____
_____
_____

8) What feedback have I received from my sponsor/mentors? _____

_____
_____
_____
_____

_____
_____
_____

9) What date will I set to complete the amends? _____
_____
_____
_____

10) Finally, what were the results of any completed amends? _____
_____
_____
_____
_____
_____
_____

    You need to pray over each amends and review it with sponsors and other mentors before actually doing anything. Make sure you re-read the principles in this step again after you have made the list and ensure you have properly applied all of the recovery principles. Let the list sit for a week or two, and then review it again.

    Mary wiped at a tear leaking from the corner of one eye before it had a chance to run across her cheek. She took a slow drink and then stared at her glass long and hard before she sat it back down. Finally she looked up at Bob and said, "It must have been really hard for you to admit to me that you were wrong. You never apologized for anything before. Ever."

    Bob just nodded his head slowly in agreement, not daring to meet her gaze.

    "I've heard about this amends thing you're doing, you know." Her voice had lost it's edginess. I understand what you are trying to do. I had a friend go through A.A. and she told me all about her amends work. I never saw you drinking much, but you're obviously in some program. What was it, cocaine?" she asked.

    Bob shifted uncomfortably in his seat. He took a sip of his own drink while he collected his thoughts. "No, not cocaine. I was never much into drugs of any kind." He continued, "I was mainly into sex. My problem is sex. Actually, the program says it is lust that I have a problem with, not sex per se. I've learned that lust is not sexual in nature, it is spiritual. You know, you can lust after people, but you can also lust after cars, jobs, houses, power, money, anything really. So its not really about sex. It's about having a false god, an idol, at the center of your life rather than Jesus Christ."

"Oh don't tell me you've gone and got religion!" exclaimed Mary.

"No," he laughed. "I'm not religious. I am very interested, however, in learning more about the life of the man named Jesus who was from Nazareth. I do believe that He was, or rather is, the son of God, who died on the cross for my sins – for all of our sins, Mary – and who rose again on the third day. Since I learned that He is God and I am not, I seem to be getting along much better in my life. Look, I've even learned that I'm not better than everyone else, and that other people's feelings do matter: Like yours, for example. That's why I'm here, Mary. I'm here to apologize for treating you the way I did, and to ask you to forgive me. Oh, and part of my amends is to restore things as much as I can to the way they were before. I know there are some things I cannot repair, but…well, when I left, I had a bunch of your CDs in my car. I have most of them here, but I think I've lost two or three, so here's a gift card…you can replace them or whatever." Bob slid the small stack of discs with the gift card on top across the table to Mary. "So, will you please forgive me, Mary?"

Mary stared at the discs with her mouth slightly hanging open. "You brought my music back?" she commented. "I thought you tossed them or maybe gave them to your next girlfriend."

Bob chuckled, "Yea, I guess that's exactly the type of thing I would have done. I wish I could claim some really cool motive, but I can't. I just had them in a box when I moved and never unpacked them."

Mary took a deep breath and exhaled loudly. "I wish I could accept your apology and give you my forgiveness. I need to think it over, ok? I wasn't really expecting all this. I guess when you told me you wanted to get together to apologize I figured you were going to try to hit on me again. I was all set to bite your head off. I had this whole long speech prepared and now…I'm not sure how to react to this…this…new you."

"Sure, I get it, Mary. I had hoped…well, I suppose all things considered, I do still have my head." He laughed. "I understand you need some time to think it over." Bob pushed his chair back from the table and reached for his wallet. He tossed some cash on the table and said, "Thank you, so much for taking the time to meet with me. I do appreciate it. If you decide you want to talk some more, you know how to reach me, ok? Lunch is on me. I've left enough for desert and the tip. Stay awhile and enjoy yourself."

As Bob walked towards the door, he heard Mary's voice behind him. "Bob?" she called with a softness to her voice.

He turned. "Yea?" he said.

"Thanks. Really…thank you." she said.

"You are welcome, Mary." he replied, and he turned back towards the door.

"Everything to your satisfaction today?" asked the waitress as he passed the front counter.

"Could have been worse." Bob tossed at her as he stepped through the door.

Lets re-visit the issue of was Mary harmed by Bob's amends. What do you think now? Certainly the conversation ended much better than it began. Do you think Mary feels better now? What do you think changed for Mary as a result of Bob's amends?

Systems Check

Do you think you're ready to start making amends now? Sorry, not just yet. Those who have gone before us have learned that we need to do a serious emotion-check before we launch into an amends. The real prospect of making an amends to someone can launch many different emotions. We may find ourselves very nervous, anxious, guilty, afraid, or overwhelmed by the anticipation of such a meeting. Many times we have found that amendees respond with an abundance of grace and understanding, making our amends a truly healing experience for everyone. Other times, however, our amendees respond with profound anger, shock or disbelief. Whatever the outcome, prior to entering the meeting, we must let go of all of our expectations of their response. Only when we have let go of our own expectations of their reactions will we be in a position to truly hear what they have to say to us.

Go back through your list of amendees. Ask yourself the following questions for each person.

1) Do I have any expectations about their reactions? _____

_____
_____
_____
_____
_____
_____
_____
_____

2) What are those expectations? _____

_____
_____
_____
_____
_____
_____
_____
_____

3) How do my expectations serve to protect me? _____
_____
_____
_____
_____
_____
_____
_____

4) How will letting go of my expectations help me? _____
_____
_____
_____
_____
_____
_____
_____
_____

5) Am I willing to accept the consequences? _____
_____
_____
_____
_____
_____
_____
_____
_____
_____

Peace

"...so far as it depends on you, be at peace with all men."

— Romans 12:18

Working through our Ninth Step is supposed to bring some sense of relief from the terrible burden of guilt we have carried around with us for so long. Like laborers who have dropped the loads from their shoulders, we often feel lighter, freer, and even physically stronger. A new sense of happiness and optimism replaces the depressed and pessimistic view of old. We must be careful not to lead with our newfound joy in our amends sessions, or else we may come across as insincere and fake. There may come a time when we can share the joy of our growth with our amendees, but it is most assuredly not when we are attempting to make amends for our wrongs against them.

As Bob drove home he realized he felt incredibly energized and somewhat tired at the same time. He was almost giddy. "Thank you, Jesus!" he shouted at is dashboard. "Wow! What do you know, confession really is good for the soul!" As the miles passed by outside his window, a small quiet place began to grow inside of Bob. He had never felt so quiet on the inside, so peaceful. He didn't even have his stereo on. He just drove his car and talked to Jesus off and on, all the way back to his hometown. Bob finally understood why the program puts so much importance on restoring our rightness with our fellow man.

Ok, now are you ready? Here's your final systems check:

❏ Are you certain of the nature of your wrong?

❏ Are you certain of the nature of the amends you will make?

❏ Does your amends focus on your part only?

❏ Does your amends begin by asking for permission to make the amends? (If not, make sure you set up the amends session so the person has made a fully 'informed consent' to receiving your amends. Otherwise, postpone or cancel the amends.)

❏ Are you fully ready to accept responsibility for what you have done?

❏ Are you fully ready to accept responsibility for what you will say?

❏ Are you willing to accept the consequences?

❏ Have you jettisoned your expectations for a specific response from your amendee?

❏ Have you turned the entire situation over to God?

❏ Have you devoted sufficient time in prayer and meditation to this specific amends?

❏ Have you adequately prepared your emotions, and your perspectives so that you can approach your amendee in humility?

Write out your amends and review it with sponsor and accountability partner. Pray over it and sit on it for at least a week or two. Then read it again and consider all the checklist questions before moving forward.

If the checklist is complete, then all systems are go!

May the wisdom and grace of Our Lord be upon you and your amendees as you continue to walk the path of humility.

Step Ten

Continued to take personal inventory and when we were wrong promptly admitted it.

> "It takes a brave man to look into the mirror of his own soul to see written there the disfigurements caused by his own misbehavior."
>
> — Fulton J. Sheen

Sharon glanced at the clock on her desk. "Ok, I have enough time to call Karan before she goes to lunch", she thought to herself. She hit the speed dial digit on her phone assigned to Karan; number 3, right after her husband and her mom.

Karan answered, "Sharon! It is good to hear from you. How are you today?"

"Really good, Karan. I wanted to thank you again for your time over these past few months and walking me through all this stuff. I can't believe how different everything is for me now. When I first started working the steps, you kept telling me over and over that things would get better if I just "keep on keeping on" and to take things "one day at a time." I don't think I ever really believed you!" she said as she laughed out loud.

"I know, Sharon. You have worked very hard! But I want you to remember that this is only the beginning and it gets even better from here! How has your work on your daily inventory been going this week?" she asked.

"Well, that's why I'm calling. I've been working the checklist you gave me, every night, just like you said to. I'm having trouble with the question about naming two things I did well today." said Sharon.

"Ok, what's the problem?" asked Karan.

"First, I feel silly writing down good things about myself. Second, I'm not sure what the point is. Isn't that like being prideful? I thought that was a sin?" Sharon asked.

"Not at all," said Karan. "But I do know what you mean. I felt silly when I first started writing down good things about myself. My sponsor told me I reacted that way because I wasn't 'comfortable' with positives about me. I was used to focusing on all my negatives, and I just had to get used to the experience of letting positives stick. She was right. I'm not so comfortable with the idea that I may do something well from time to time," She chuckled.

"Oh, I see," said Sharon. "Well that probably makes sense for me too. I even crack jokes when other people try and pay me a compliment."

"Exactly," agreed Karan. "It turns out that getting used to acknowledging our own positives is part of the point in doing this exercise. Your question about pride is a very good one. Sinful pride is the love of the self. It is to love yourself more than God or others. Our program teaches us the concept of 'accurate esteem', which means to be able to perceive ourselves accurately and to value, or esteem, ourselves accordingly. Therefore, unless we can see the fullness of truth about ourselves, our character defects AND our character assets, we cannot accurately esteem ourselves. Accurate esteem for our selves is also important because it enables us to accurately esteem others: to not care for others more than we should, or less than we should. That always leads us into relationship problems. So acknowledging our positives is not the same thing as ignoring our negatives. Makes sense?" finished Karan.

"Wow, Karan, that's a lot to digest all at once," said Sharon. "I think I understand what you're saying about sinful pride versus accurate esteem. I'm making some notes here so I can think more about it later. I know you have to get to lunch, so I'll let you go. Thanks so much for the input. I'll call you tomorrow."

"Just when I was thinking I was done with the majority of the work in this program! Ha!" thought Sharon as she hung up the phone. "The easy part may be behind me!"

Little did we know, when we first embarked upon our journey with these steps, that it would take this long, be this hard, or require as much work as it has. Little did we know that this journey has no end. That's right: We never actually finish the steps, or at least not in the sense that we stop working them. The steps are comprised of two types: 1) Those that help us achieve sobriety, and 2) Those steps that help us maintain our sobriety.

Step Ten is the first of the "maintenance steps." Steps Ten, Eleven, and Twelve are the guides for helping us keep the sobriety we worked so hard to achieve. Steps One through Nine are all about getting sober and dealing with the damage caused by our addiction. Changed by this work in ways we could not have imagined, we have become what Alcoholics Anonymous describes as "good citizens"— more humble, honest, and aware of the thoughts and feelings of others than we would have thought possible. We have endured a thorough scrubbing, inside and out; sort of like taking a good hot shower. However, every day, we walk through our lives and we get a little, or a lot, dirty again. We get frustrated with the tasks of life, hurt by the words or actions of others, disappointed in our selves, and perhaps even lose touch with our connection with God. Remembering that we are addicts, capable of going back to our old ways, we fight to stay "clean" in an entirely new way. The maintenance steps help us to "freshen up" again, so we do not become crusted over and lose our sobriety.

Those who came before us along this journey of recovery have taught us that taking our personal inventory is best done on a regular, daily basis.

...*personal inventory*...

Step Ten repeats the work we began in Steps Four through Nine, but this time we only have to deal with today, or the past few days if we have been negligent, instead of having to deal with EVERYTHING that came before the moment we started our Fourth Step work. In sobriety we learn to remain focused on this moment and live in today.

To begin with the obvious, the "personal" part of "personal inventory" means that we work on our own defects and shortcomings, not someone else's. Additionally, it refers us to our personal, as opposed to business, strengths and weaknesses. To inventory the fact that we may be organizationally challenged, or that we excel at accounting, is not the primary objective here. We should be focusing on our character assets and our character defects. Some of those may evidence themselves in our business relationships, and in that event that would be an appropriate item to include in our personal inventory.

What is an inventory? In its original usage, an inventory was a list of goods and materials held available in stock by a business. Thanks to A.A., it has come to refer to a tally of the "goods and materials" of our personhood. Specifically, we tally everything: thoughts, feelings and behaviors. We take stock of things we did, and things we didn't do, things we said, and things we should have said but did not, and things we felt, or things we ought to have had some feelings about but did not.

We have provided a sample inventory at the end of this guide to help you get started. This worksheet is a resource that you can draw from to create your own daily inventory that works best for you. There are more items in our list than you would need to use every day, in fact, some items are repeated, stated in a different ways. Choose the items that best help you tally your thoughts, feelings, and behaviors for a given day.

> *"But exhort one another daily, while it is called 'Today,' lest any of you be hardened by the deceitfulness of sin."*
>
> — *Hebrews 3:13*

Why should we take a daily inventory?

As addicts it is far too easy for us to walk way down the slippery slope before we realize the danger we are in, unless we are diligent and thorough with our daily inventory. The Tenth Step helps us to stay aware of our "stinkin' thinkin'" and associated negative feelings, so we can change our direction before we get ourselves into trouble.

In Hebrews, Paul advises us to exhort one another daily so that we do not become "...hardened by the deceitfulness of sin." Those who have walked the path of recovery before us teach us that this disease is "cunning and baffling". It creeps up on you slowly, like a lioness stalking her prey, moving so slowly that we don't really notice the changes, until it is far too late. The analogy has limited utility in regards to sin because sin, for the most part, is not an external source stalking us. Rather it is an internal struggle of our minds.

> *When tempted, no one should say, "God is tempting me." For God cannot be tempted by evil, nor does he tempt anyone; but each one is tempted when, by his own evil desire, he is dragged away and enticed. Then, after desire has conceived, it gives birth to sin, and sin, when it is full-grown, gives birth to death."*
>
> — *James 1: 13-15*

We first visited this issue of temptation in Step Three. This is so important that it is worth revisiting. James 1:13-15 is one of the most important verses in the Bible. It tells us something very important about the nature of sin: It identifies the source of all temptation. It is not, as some would assert, the Devil. Neither is it God. What exactly is a temptation? Is it really a thought inserted in your head by some outside power? What if that outside power suggested you jump off the roof? Would you be tempted? Probably not. The key is this: You cannot be tempted by something that is not tempting **to you**. In other words, the source of the temptation lies within your own beliefs and perspectives about a thing. For example, if someone were to suggest that you set your head on fire, you probably would not be tempted to do so, believing that setting your head on fire would be a painful, potentially lethal, exercise with no good outcome either way. Therefore, if you are tempted to do something, it is because you have a belief that it would be a good thing to do, even when you know it is a wrong thing to do. That belief leads to a desire to do the thing.

We are tempted by our own "evil desires." What makes a desire evil? Simply that it is contrary to God's will for our lives. So if we have a desire that we know is sinful, how do we wind up sinning? Why doesn't righteousness automatically trump sin? Many times it does. At times, however, or in the face of particular temptations, we appear to have no brakes on the bus of sin at all. The mechanism which makes it OK for good people to do bad things is something we call "permissive beliefs" or rationalizations. For example, if I have the belief that no one will know, or it won't hurt anyone else, then I have a belief that gives me permission to do the thing I know I should not do. The "deceitfulness of sin" as Paul writes about in Hebrews is that "cunning and baffling" process of not challenging our varied forms of "stinkin' thinkin'" on a daily basis and making sure that we allow Jesus to transform our lives by renewing our minds (Romans 12:2). If we clean house daily, our house stays in order.

Take some time to re-read your work from Step Three on temptation. Make any revisions you feel may be appropriate and keep your notes close by for use in your daily inventory. If we don't stay on top of this stinkin thinkin it will stay on top of us.

Stinking Thinking

> "...and we take captive every thought to make it obedient to Christ."
>
> — 2 Corinthians 10:5

Most often, our negative emotions trigger our acting out. Somewhere in our past, we got the idea that negative emotions were unbearable and to be avoided at all costs. By working the Tenth Step, we begin to realize that negative emotions are only feelings, not crises, and that if we leave them alone we can not only survive them, but we can learn to change much of the stinkin' thinkin' that creates our negative feelings in the first place.

For example, if our boss criticized the quality of our work today, we would likely experience some negative emotions. Some of us in this situation may have the thought, "My boss doesn't appreciate all the stuff I did right today. He only saw the one thing I did wrong!" Therefore, we feel hurt, judged, or angry. We must be careful to process our thoughts thoroughly and look for any stinkin' thinkin'. Or, as Paul writes, we must "take captive every thought" and make it obedient to Christ. What does it mean to make a thought obedient to Christ? In the most direct sense it means that we must make certain that a given thought is Christ-like. Far too often we don't take the time to think about what we are thinking about, we just let our thoughts run away with us. Simply because a thought is in our head does not make it accurate or true, helpful or honest, and certainly not Godly. We must challenge each thought and shape it to be like God's thoughts.

The first thing to do is to ask ourselves several questions: "Is this thought the kind of thought that Jesus would have?" "Is it possible I am seeing only a portion of the truth in this situation?" "Am I engaging in any 'stinkin thinkin' in this situation, such as being overly sensitive or blaming others for things I am responsible for?" "Am I 'mind reading,' or assuming I know what others are thinking about me without having checked it out?"

The next thing to do is to look at our part in the situation: What did we do that was wrong, or inadequate, in our performance and what can we do to correct it? How does acknowledging our part in a situation change our initial perceptions of the situation? Here is another opportunity to shape this thought into one that is obedient to Christ.

The third step is to ask ourselves if there is another explanation (other than our original thought) for this situation that is more accurate, true, helpful, and Godly? How do we know, for example, that our boss didn't appreciate ANYTHING we did that day that was positive? Perhaps that's really true, but perhaps we are just worried that this is true. For example, perhaps our boss was having a bad day himself and therefore his reaction actually had nothing to do with us, and everything to do with him. Alternately, even if it were true that our boss thinks we are 100 percent incompetent, does that make it so? What one person thinks of us does not define us.

If we take time to process our stinkin' thinkin', challenge these distortions, and replace them with more Godly, helpful thoughts, we might actually get along better with ourselves and our fellow man. The negative emotions we originally felt will dissipate as we focus on our new thoughts. In the end we wind up being not only sober, but also genuinely content and happy people.

Are you a happy, content person today?

...and when we were wrong...

> "Therefore confess your sins to each other and pray for each other so that you may be healed. The prayer of a righteous man is powerful and effective."
>
> — James 5:16

Identifying that we are wrong is oftentimes the most difficult part for us. As addicts, we believe that we are right, even when our "wrongness" is obvious to everyone else. Be that as it may, we should not compound that wrong by not taking the time to reflect upon what we might have done, or to ask someone for feedback. Eventually, when we have settled down, if we listen carefully, we can hear our conscience knocking on our door to remind us that we had been inappropriate. Taking the time, every day, to review our experiences and make continual adjustments in our outlook is the best way to stay current, and not let things build up.

"When we were wrong" refers to errors of commission as well as errors of omission – things we do, as well as things we don't do. Therefore, we must be broadminded and think about all aspects of our personhood. For example, if I do or say something that injures someone else – yes, whether you meant to hurt them or not – if I do not make amends to them I have erred by commission (the original act that hurt the person), as well as by omission (by not making amends). Now I have two things to make amends for! See how it piles up if we don't stay current!?!

...promptly admitted it.

> *"For I say, through the grace given to me, to everyone who is among you, not to think of himself more highly than he ought to think, but to think soberly, as God has dealt to each one a measure of faith."*
>
> — *Romans 12:3*

"Promptly": Here is yet another problem for those of us with addictive natures. We don't like those nasty little negative emotions and admitting we were wrooo...that we were wrronnn...ahem...that we were wrong...can produce feelings of embarrassment and shame. To make matters worse, our program insists that we make this admission "promptly"! It is one thing to admit we were wrong about something that happened twenty years ago, and yet something else entirely to admit we were wrong about something that happened two minutes ago. Therefore, most of us have a tendency to want to avoid the "prompt" part of the Tenth Step. We must avoid avoidance, and deal with our lives in as prompt a manner as is possible in the given situation.

When we first heard this assertion, many of us challenged it, saying that if negative emotions are the triggers for acting out, shouldn't we avoid the negative emotions, so we don't act out? That rationale might actually work, were it not for one little problem: Avoiding negative emotions never gets rid of the negative emotions, they just pile up and grow into resentments. Resentments are one of the top three triggers for acting out!

The only way to the other side of pain is right down the middle; we cannot walk around it, or jump over it. There is an interesting thing that happens as we grow in our willingness and ability to stay with a negative emotion, to let it "run its course": We find that we are able to live in the present moment and to be at peace. For those of you who have not experienced peace yet, and wonder what it is, try this: imagine what it would feel like to exist without anxiety, fear, worry, anger, resentment, hate, or stress. Quiet inside, isn't it? That is peace.

> *"An expansion of the individual consciousness toward a harmony with Infinite Consciousness demands of the individual that he take on, commensurately, other characteristics of his Creator."*
>
> — *Leonare E. Read*

What benefit does the Tenth Step bring to us? Some have said that the importance of the Tenth Step lies in its ability to function as a catalyst to our continued sobriety. Some point out the benefits of learning to live in the present moment. Others have said that our continued sobriety is just the beginning. The true fruit of this labor is really our personal and spiritual growth. In the final analysis, our goal is not just to be sober, but also to become more Christ-like, every day. Therefore, every day, we must check in the mirror to see how much we look like our Savior.

A Daily Inventory

A suggested structure for a daily inventory

What follows is a list of "really good questions" that others have found helpful in working their Tenth Step. This list is not meant to be exhaustive, only suggestive, to help you develop your own Tenth Step List. Feel free to add, delete or change, as you and your sponsor see fit to achieve the goals of Step Ten.

1. What were three things that I did well today? Or things that I was good at? _____

_____

_____

_____

_____

_____

_____

_____

2. Did I stay sober today? If yes, what choices did I make and what tools did I use? (externally) _____

_____

_____

_____

_____

_____

_____

_____

3. Did I stay sober today? If yes, what choices did I make and what tools did I use? (internally) _____

_____
_____
_____
_____
_____
_____
_____
_____
_____

4. If "no" to either question one or two, what do I need to do to deal with that problem? _

_____
_____
_____
_____
_____
_____
_____
_____

5. Did I make time today to study God's Word? If yes, what was helpful about it. If no, why not and what changes do I need to make to get back on track with that priority? ____

_____
_____
_____
_____
_____
_____
_____
_____

6. Did I make time today to talk to God? If yes, what was helpful about it. If no, why not and what changes do I need to make to get back on track with that priority? _____

_____
_____
_____
_____
_____
_____
_____
_____
_____

7. Did I make time today to listen to God? If yes, what was helpful about it. If no, why not and what changes do I need to make to get back on track with that priority? _____

_____
_____
_____
_____
_____
_____
_____
_____
_____

8. Did I do anything today to serve others? If yes, what was helpful about it. If no, why not and what changes do I need to make to get back on track with that priority? _____

_____
_____
_____
_____
_____
_____
_____
_____
_____

9. Did I practice contentment in my life today or did I indulge my sense of self-pity or entitlement? If yes, what was helpful about it. If no, why not and what changes do I need to make to get back on track with that priority? _____

_____
_____
_____
_____
_____
_____
_____
_____
_____

10. In what ways did I remove God from the center of my life today? _____

_____
_____
_____
_____
_____
_____
_____
_____

11. During my day today, did I spend too much time "futurizing" or "past-urizing" (obsessing on the future or the past)? _____

_____
_____
_____
_____
_____
_____
_____

12. Did I obsess on any person or object today? If yes, what and what did obsessing about that person/thing do for me? _____

_____
_____
_____
_____
_____
_____
_____
_____
_____

13. Did I invite the Holy Spirit to fill me today and minister to me? (2 Peter 3:18) If yes, what was helpful about it. If no, why not and what changes do I need to make to get back on track with that priority _____

_____
_____
_____
_____
_____
_____
_____
_____
_____

14. Did I experience anything that was upsetting to me today? What happened? _____

_____
_____
_____
_____
_____
_____
_____
_____
_____

15. If yes, what negative emotions did I experience? _____

_____
_____
_____
_____
_____
_____
_____
_____
_____

16. If yes, what thoughts did I wrestle with and did I deal appropriately with them? If yes, how and if no, what how did not dealing with them appropriately affect me? What do I need to do next time to handle my thoughts appropriately? _____

_____
_____
_____
_____
_____
_____
_____
_____
_____

17. What character defects played a part in my life today? _____

_____
_____
_____
_____
_____
_____
_____
_____
_____

18. Did I do anything or say anything today that I wish I had not done or said? What? __

_____
_____
_____
_____
_____
_____
_____
_____
_____

19. Did I NOT do or say anything today that I wish I HAD said or done? What? _____

_____
_____
_____
_____
_____
_____
_____
_____
_____

20. Did I notice any of my old behaviors today? If yes, what were they? _____

_____
_____
_____
_____
_____
_____
_____
_____
_____

21. Did any of my old stinkin' thinkin' emerge today? If yes, what were the distorted thoughts I struggled with? _____

_____
_____
_____
_____
_____
_____
_____
_____
_____

22. What evidence was there to support my thought? _____

_____
_____
_____
_____
_____
_____
_____
_____
_____

23. What evidence was there that did NOT support my thought? _____

_____
_____
_____
_____
_____
_____
_____
_____
_____

24. If my friend was in this situation and had this thought what would I tell him or her? Is that what I am saying to myself? _____

_____
_____
_____
_____
_____
_____
_____
_____
_____

25. What would be a more helpful thought to have in this situation? _____

_____
_____
_____
_____
_____
_____
_____
_____
_____

26. Did I properly work my program today? Evaluate._____

_____
_____
_____
_____
_____
_____
_____
_____
_____

27. Did I avoid working any part of my program today? If yes, what part and what do I need to do to correct that? _____

_____
_____
_____
_____
_____
_____
_____
_____
_____
_____

28. Did I experience any of the following emotions today?

- ❏ Resentment
- ❏ Fatigue
- ❏ Hurt
- ❏ Loneliness
- ❏ Disappointment
- ❏ Fear
- ❏ Anger
- ❏ Frustration

29. How can changing my thoughts alter the negative emotions I experienced?

_____
_____
_____
_____
_____
_____
_____
_____
_____
_____

30. Take three minutes to take several slow, deep breaths, relaxing all the muscles in your body, and then visualize yourself lying on the beach, focusing completely on that image and ignoring all other input. At the end of the three minutes, what happened to your negative emotions? Did they get worse, better, or stay the same? What do you learn from this exercise about negative emotions? _____

_____
_____

_____
_____
_____
_____
_____
_____
_____

31. Did I demonstrate any of the following behaviors today?

    ❏ selfishness   ❏ self-centeredness
    ❏ dishonesty   ❏ withdrawal/isolation
    ❏ whining   ❏ short-temper/irritability
    ❏ gossiping   ❏ demeaning others
    ❏ avoidance   ❏ aggressiveness
    ❏ workaholism   ❏ passive-aggressiveness

32. Today, did I experience any lustful thoughts? _____
_____
_____
_____
_____
_____
_____
_____
_____
_____

33. If yes, did I take appropriate steps to deal with them? _____
_____
_____
_____
_____
_____
_____
_____

34. If I did not take appropriate steps, why not? _____

35. What corrective action do I need to take tomorrow? _____

36. Did anything happen today that I am reluctant to tell my sponsor and/or accountability partners? _____

37. If yes, why, and what do I plan to do about it? _____

_____
_____
_____
_____
_____
_____
_____
_____

38. What blessings were in my life today? (be sure to start with the basics, such as being alive, fed, sheltered, and work your way up from there). _____

_____
_____
_____
_____
_____
_____
_____
_____

39. Am I allowing myself to be truly grateful for those blessings today? If yes, then say a prayer and thank God for those blessings. If no, what is in the way for you? Go back and rework your Tenth Step until you can find your gratitude, and then thank God for His blessings. _____

_____
_____
_____
_____
_____
_____
_____
_____

Step Eleven

Sought through prayer and meditation to improve our relationship with God, praying for knowledge of His will for us, and the power to carry that out.

> "The fewer the words, the better the prayer."
>
> — *Martin Luther*

Bob's hand fumbled about in the semi-dark room for the buzzing alarm clock for a moment before he found the offensive little piece of technology. Resisting the temptation to fling it across the room, he pressed the off button and sat it back down, with enthusiasm, upon the nightstand.

"It's too early to get up!" he thought loudly inside his head. He rolled over and pulled a pillow on top of his head.

"Why did I ever promise Dwight that I would do this!?!" he whined.

"Because he convinced you that it wasn't all that hard and would be 'really' good for you to do. That's why," he answered.

Bob flung the pillow and covers off and headed towards the bathroom. After taking care of business he brushed his teeth and splashed some cold water on his face. Returning to his bed, he resisted the urge to crawl back under the covers and instead, dropped to his knees, and rested his head upon the side of his mattress.

"Lord," he began. "I don't know if you are up yet or not, but I guess I am, so what-do-ya-say, wanna talk for a bit?"

Bob talked to God for a good four, or maybe five, minutes, and then found he had run out of things to say. "I wonder if I should pray for world peace of something like that" he muttered to himself. He stood up, grabbed his Bible from the nightstand and jumped onto the bed in a seated position. He opened the Bible to his marker in the book of Mark. He began reading in the fifth chapter at the 24th verse:

...a large crowd followed and pressed around him. And a woman was there who had been subject to bleeding for twelve years. She had suffered a great deal under the care of many doctors and had spent all she had, yet instead of getting better she grew worse. When she heard about Jesus, she came up behind him in the crowd and touched his cloak, because she thought, "If I just touch his clothes, I will be healed.' Immediately her bleeding stopped and she felt in her body that she was freed from her suffering.

At once Jesus realized that power had gone out from him. He turned around in the crowd and asked, "Who touched my clothes?"

"You see the people crowding against you," his disciples answered, "and yet you can ask, 'Who touched me?'"

But Jesus kept looking around to see who had done it."

Then the woman, knowing what had happened to her, came and fell at his feet and, trembling with fear, told him the whole truth.

He said to her, "Daughter, your faith has healed you. Go in peace and be freed from your suffering."

— Mark 5:21-32

Bob was vaguely aware of an intensity of focus and stillness within him. He re-read the same passage letting the scene play out again in his mind's eye. He could almost smell the dust of the street kicked up by the feet of the crowd and hear their buzz as Jesus pronounced the woman healed.

He had so many thoughts rushing around his head, "Why didn't Jesus know who touched his cloak? Why were the disciples so disrespectful to him? Why was the woman so afraid after she had been healed? Why was she healed without him actively doing the healing, like when he put mud on the eyes of the blind man to heal him? He didn't even talk to her!"

He reread the passage again, looking for answers.

"Ah ha!, that's one answer," Bob thought to himself as he read verse 34, "…your FAITH has healed you."

"So it was the woman's 'faith' that healed her. It was her belief that Jesus was the Son of God, that he had the power to heal her, that's what did it?" Bob thought aloud.

"So if I have that kind of faith, will God heal me?" Bob wondered.

"Lord Jesus," Bob began in prayer. "I do not know if I understand how all of this healing business works, but I want, desperately to be healed from my sexual addiction. If I could touch the hem of your robe, I would. Amen."

Bob put away his Bible and began to get ready to go to work. He suddenly noticed that he was not in the least bit tired, in fact, he felt more energized than he did on most mornings that he could recall.

"Well, Dwight was right after all: It wasn't really all that hard to get up early to spend a little time with God, and it feels like it was a really good thing for me this morning. I didn't figure out the answers to all of my questions, but I bet Dwight knows somebody who can help me with them." Bob thought to himself. He was also aware that he didn't really feel "healed in his body" like the woman did, but he definitely felt good.

"I think I'll do this again tomorrow," he thought.

We have traveled a long road to this point in our step work. When we first entered this program we were battered and bleeding from the abuses we inflicted upon ourselves, and those who dared to love us. Many of us were sure there was no God, or if there was, we were He. Others of us believed in God, but concluded that there must be something defective about us, since we were unable to live according to His standards, standards that every other Christian seemed to be able to keep. We believed we were alone in our struggle; and in our aloneness, we were lost.

The "longest walk," as it has been described, is that first walk from our car to the doorway of our first meeting. When we entered that room of recovery, we could hardly meet anyone's gaze. Head down we skulked to the coffee table, or the darkest corner of the room where we might go unnoticed. Some of us experienced an overwhelming flood of shame and guilt in those first few moments. Others of us felt a wave of relief realizing the room was not empty.

Step One spoke the truth we already knew about ourselves, that our lives had become unmanageable. Steps Two and Three helped us to realize that God was on our side, if we let Him. And Steps Four through Ten helped us to learn how to become more Christ-like and stay sober at the same time. Step Eleven is about maturing as Christians, moving from our ego-centric former lives, to an other-centered, Christ-like existence.

Step Eleven teaches us how to improve our relationship with God. It instructs us in the vehicle that carries us (seeking Him) and on what roads (prayer and meditation) we should drive. There is an often-repeated story of Martin Luther's phenomenal discipline in his relationship with God. It is said that Martin would get up every morning at 4 am and pray for two hours before he started his day. One of his students asked him, "Martin, how is it that you are able to get up so early and pray for so long every single day?!" Martin replied simply, "I get up, I get down on my knees, and I pray!"

Sought...

> *"I love those who love me, and those who seek me find me."*
>
> — *Proverbs 8:17*

The truth of the matter is that as long as we believed we were self-sufficient, we had no need to seek another God. We were the masters of our own ship and we suffered no one else telling us what to do. To acknowledge that God exists would surely lead to the surrender of our glorious vessel and all of our power and control. Perhaps He would exile us to a life as a missionary in the Congo, or a life of poverty, or worse yet, a life without sex! Little did we understand the true nature of God. Eventually, broken and bankrupt, we found we had no place to turn, and we sought him out. We searched for Him. We called out to the darkness and said, "God, if you are there, please help me." How much we have changed since that moment, how much we have learned in these past few months about who God is, and who He is not.

...through prayer and meditation...

> *"Be still, and know that I am God."*
>
> — *Psalm 46:10*

We have heard it said that prayer is talking to God, and meditation is listening to God. Many of us were practiced at talking to God, but few of us had ever spent much time listening to Him. How blessed we were to learn that not only would God listen to us, but He would also talk to us in return! We simply have to learn how to listen!

1. Did you spend time listening to God today? _____

2. If you did, what did He have to say to you?_____

3. How did listening to God help you today?_____

4. If you did not, what did you miss out on? _____

Still others have defined meditation as "to think intently and at length, as for spiritual purposes." (Dictionary.com). The Eleventh Step helps us to develop a deeper and more meaningful relationship with God by thinking intently about Him and His Word. In those quiet moments of meditation, we sometimes hear God teaching us, helping us to understand His Word in a way we never dreamed possible. Only by taking the time to be quiet and to listen to Him did we find that God had a lot to say.

...to improve our relationship with God...

> *"You will seek me and find me when you seek me with all your heart."*
>
> — *Jeremiah 29:13*

Did you notice the reference to our "relationship" with God? Many of us are not accustomed to thinking of God as someone to "relate" to. We would consider him someone to talk to, especially when we are trouble, but how does a finite being actually relate to an infinite being? Somehow, we imagine it as being impossible. Yet, God insists that it is not only possible, but actually, it is what He prefers.

Consider your relationship with God during the past week. How much time did you spend with God last week, not counting church — assuming you went? How much time did you spend praying and how much time listening? How much time did you spend reading, studying, or meditating on His word? Now, tally that all up and compare how much time did you spend with your best friend, or your spouse, or your coworkers? If your spouse gave you the same amount of time to you as you give to God, would you be happy with it?

Those who have gone before us in this program teach us that the best way to develop or improve our relationship with God is to work at it every day. They tell us that every day we need to pray some, to read His word some, and to spend some time listening to him. Additionally, and on a regular basis, we need to fellowship with other believers, to worship with other believers, and to spend time studying the Bible.

How much time should we spend with God? Generally, we recommend that we have some time every day to pray and read the Bible, and at least every week to fellowship and worship. When you set your goal for this commitment, make sure you choose a goal that you actually will do. For example, it may sound great to pray for an hour every day first thing in the morning; however, many of us cannot make ourselves get up early enough to make that happen. Perhaps it may be better to commit to praying for five minutes every day and succeed at that, rather than to commit to an hour a day and fail. If you succeed at the five minutes a day goal, you can always build on that success and choose a longer goal. Whatever goals you choose, write them out and then go over them with your accountability partners and sponsor. Ask for their feedback on how "doable" the goals sound to them, and their help in keeping you accountable to your goals.

...praying for knowledge of His will for us...

> *"Do not conform any longer to the pattern of this world, but be transformed by the renewing of your mind. Then you will be able to test and approve what God's will is – His good, pleasing and perfect will."*
>
> — *Romans 12:2*

Can anyone fathom the mind of God? How does anyone really "know" what God's will is? Yet, the Scriptures insist that we can know what God's will is for us. In his letter to the church at Rome, Paul defines the formula for us: Allow God to change (transform) our patterns of thought according to His pattern, and then we will be able to know His will. If you want to know God's will for you, you must let Him shape your mind.

Allowing our minds to be transformed by God is the hard part. We must surrender our will daily. We must allow our thoughts to be replaced by His thoughts. We can only accomplish this by establishing a discipline in our life. Pray at specific times, and maintain an attitude of prayer constantly. Study the Word. Meditate. Worship some. Repeat daily.

God reveals His will to us in many different ways. He speaks to us through His word, the Holy Bible. Sometimes He speaks to us through other people or circumstances. At other times, He speaks to us in that still quiet voice in the back of our heads that none but us can hear. Occasionally, He still speaks out loud in that audible voice that makes you turn your head to see who is there, when no one is. Whatever method He chooses, God will tell us exactly what we need to know exactly when we need to know it.

Take a few moments to look up the following verse: Jeremiah 29:11. Write the passage in the space provided: Jeremiah 29:11 _____

_____

_____

_____

_____

What does this verse have todo with you? Re-write the verse, inserting your name wherever the word "you" appears. _____

_____

_____

_____

_____

When we ask ourselves, or others, the question: "What is God's will for your life?" we often overlook the obvious answers. For example, we know that God wants us to be in relationship with Him in this life and to spend eternity with Him in the next (John 3:16). That is an example of "Special Revelation," or knowledge that comes from a supernatural source, such as the Bible. Another source of knowledge about God's will comes from "General Revelation" such as common sense or the study of natural sciences such as medicine or physics. For example, we know that God wants us to be active because medical research shows that people who lead active lifestyles are generally physically and emotionally more healthy than those who lead sedentary lifestyles.

A common question people ask is "What should I be 'doing' with my life?" By that question, they are often asking what job or career they should have, or perhaps whether they should be involved in a ministry in some way. Addressing that question is beyond the scope of this guide, but we can refer you to The Purpose Driven Life, by Rick Warren as a good step in that direction.

1. What do you know about God's will for your life? What was revealed to you by general revelation and what by special revelation?

a. General Revelation: _____

_____
_____
_____
_____
_____

b. Special Revelation: _____

_____
_____
_____
_____
_____
_____

2. How will working the eleventh step help you understand God's will for your life better? _____

_____
_____
_____
_____
_____

...and the power to carry that out.

> "And when they had prayed, the place where they were assembled together was shaken; and they were all filled with the Holy Spirit, and they spoke the word of God with boldness."
> — Acts 4:31

It is one thing to know God's will for us, and yet another thing to carry it out. In this situation, the word "power" can mean many different things. It can mean: ability, strength, integrity, willingness, energy, resources, courage, faith, humility, commitment, eagerness, compassion, sense of justice, perseverance, fortitude, patience, honesty, assertiveness, humor, foresight, or intuition. One or more of these characteristics or qualities may be required of us in order to carry out God's will in our lives. So when you pray for knowledge of God's will for your life, also pray for whatever it is you will need to carry His will out.

1. What part of God's will for your life do you currently lack the power to carry out? ___

_____
_____
_____
_____
_____
_____
_____
_____

2. Write here your prayer to ask God to remedy the above weakness: _____

_____
_____
_____
_____
_____
_____
_____

Another definition of the term, "power," can refer to the fuel that gets the work done. The gas in your tank, for example, powers your car down the road. Without it the car has no power and goes nowhere. Are you running on a full tank of gas? In the spiritual sense of this word, the power is the Holy Spirit. If you want to be used by God, then you need to be continuously filled with the Holy Spirit (Ephesians 5:18). It is sort of like how the wind fills the sails of a ship at sea and carries it along to where it needs to go. If you are filled with the Holy Spirit, fulfilling God's will for your life will be easy, in the sense that you will always know which way the wind is blowing, making your direction clear.

Having a full tank of fuel is a prerequisite for action. The ability to put one foot in front of the other and convert that fuel into action is another matter. We have to develop a number of character assets to follow God's plan: humility, obedience, and faith. Why do we need these three assets? We need these three in particular because they are all three interdependent, one upon the other. Without them, we will be too proud, too rebellious, or too frightened to carry out God's will. With them, God can change the world.

Humility is required to keep our egos in check. We have to remember that it is not about us. It is not even done by us, neither is it done in our own strength or ability. It is all about God, for His glory, and by His power and strength. We are only the piano player; we are neither composer nor the piano itself. What are we then? That's the easy part: We are the obedient servant, following our master's instructions.

The character asset of "obedience" is the second gear for developing some momentum. Do you remember the story of Jonah? God instructed him to go to the city of Nineva (see the book of Jonah for the whole story) to preach to the residents about how wicked they had become. Jonah, lacking the character asset of obedience, ran the other way. God used a storm and a large fish to help Jonah build his character! Fear is a result of failing to trust in God's plan for us and to see the situation through God's eyes.

The final asset, faith, is the knowledge or awareness of who God is, who we are, and how, in this moment, we are following His plan. The Book of Hebrews defines faith as the "assurance of things hoped for, the conviction of things unseen." When we are convinced of the rightness of the next thing for us to do, and we are humbly obedient to take that step, we experience a peace and serenity unlike any other moment we can have.

"As it is the business of tailors to make clothes and of cobblers to mend shoes, so it is the business of Christians to pray."

— *Martin Luther*

On the next page you will find a recommended tool for strengthening your spirituality. It is just a calendar, to help you track different behaviors related to spirituality. In our example, we track prayer, reading the Bible and attending church. There may be additional aspects of spirituality you want to track such as attending a Bible study.

Strengthening Spirituality Calendar

In the sample calendar provided, we have offered a suggested routine for increasing spiritual strength. As little as thirty minutes a day can really make a difference. For space reasons, we've abbreviated the activities.

P 10 m = pray for ten minutes
R 10 m = read the Bible for ten minutes

	Sunday	Monday	Tuesday	Wednesday	Thursday	Friday	Saturday
6					P 10 m	P 10 m	P 10 m
7	P 10 m	P 10 m	P 10 m	P 10 m			
8							
9							
10	church						
11	church						
12	church	R 10 m	R 10 m	R 10 m	R 10 m	R 10 m	R 10 m
1							
2							
3							
4							
5				Bible study			
6				Bible study			
7							
8							
9							
10	P 10 m	P 10 m	P 10 m	P 10 m	P 10 m	P 10 m	P 10 m
11							

In the blank calendar provided below, schedule your spiritual activities for the coming week. Reminder: Make your goals "doable" ones, so that you will do them! Once you've succeeded you can always increase the goals, but start with what you will do.

For example, for the first week or two, you might set a goal to pray for 3 minutes. After you've succeeded at that, you might set the goal for the next two weeks to pray for 5 minutes. When you set goals that are perfectly doable, you accomplish then, and then you get to build on success! After you've worked up your first calendar, share it with your accountability partners and sponsor and ask for their feedback.

	Sunday	Monday	Tuesday	Wednesday	Thursday	Friday	Saturday
6							
7							
8							
9							
10							
11							
12							
1							
2							
3							
4							
5							
6							
7							
8							
9							
10							
11							

Perfection

For those of us who struggle with perfectionist or legalistic tendencies, we need to apply a healthy dose of grace to the times when we are unable to have a Daily Walk. That's right. Some days we choose not to, or we forget, or we don't do everything we know is best for us. Sometimes life just gets in the way. As our fellow travelers in recovery are fond of saying, "Stuff happens." How do we handle these imperfections? We acknowledge that we didn't get it done, look for any particular reasons we may be avoiding spending time with God, and we get back to it the next day. As addicts, we tend to behave in "black or white" or "all or nothing" ways; so we tend to use one forgotten quiet time as an excuse to stop doing them all together. As recovering addicts, we learn how to live in the gray zone in the middle. We accept the reality of our imperfection and carry on with the program, in spite of the fact that we messed up. We "keep on keeping on." Remember that God is never farther away than your own thoughts. If you forget to do your quiet time before you leave, talk to God on your way to work!

Step Twelve

Having had a spiritual awakening as the result of these steps, we tried to carry this message to other lust addicts, and to practice these principles in all our affairs.

"Kindness has converted more people than zeal, science, or eloquence."

— Mother Teresa

"Ohhh, what have I gotten myself into?" Sharon thought to herself as she exited her car and headed towards the church building.

She thought back to the conversation she had just a few hours earlier with her sponsor and reminded herself of Karan's advice. "Just be yourself, tell your story, and let God do everything else," She had said. "It sounded a whole lot easier last night," Sharon grumbled to herself.

She rounded the corner and stopped in her tracks as she saw the crowd of people milling about outside and inside the meeting room. It was going to be a packed house. She was contemplating turning around and scurrying away when she heard Karan's voice, "Hey Sharon! Come on over here, I want you to meet somebody."

"Great", she thought to herself. "Doesn't Karan know I'm stressed about sharing my story tonight? The LAST thing I need is to have to meet somebody I don't know!"

She obediently walked over, and Karan said, "Sharon, this is Latisha. Latisha, this is Sharon."

Sharon extended her hand and shook Latisha's, finding it a little cool and clammy. Latisha offered Sharon a weak, nervous smile and her eyes glanced downward quickly after making initial contact. Sharon's stomach did a little flip as she recognized the look of fear and lostness in Latisha's eyes. She thought, "I must have had that same look on my face the first night I came to this meeting."

Her heart went out to her and she said, "Hi Latisha, I am so glad you are here tonight!" She extended her arms and gave her a warm hug. "Let's go inside and find you some tea and a muffin, ok?"

Karan smiled as she watched the two women walk inside the room. "She's going to be just fine," she thought to herself.

What was it that made the difference for each of us when we came to program? For some of us it was hearing the stories of others who had been where we were and had been able to get and stay sober. For others it was the warmth and fellowship of those who greeted us, and how they treated each other. For still others it was the encouragements liberally given to us by the old timers. How many different facets were there to the hope that we found? In short, we witnessed others living out the Twelfth Step for us to see. Each week we saw their kindness towards us, in spite of our continued failures, and we studied their examples of how they worked their program. We witnessed the grace of Jesus Christ and knew we could hope for that for ourselves as well.

Having had a spiritual awakening...

What is a "spiritual awakening"? It is the emerging awareness of our spirituality – realizing that we are spiritual beings. Our awakening began when we came to the first step, realizing we were not all-powerful but powerless. Our awakening continued with the second step when we realized there is a God who loves us and wants to be in a daily intimate relationship with us. For some of us it happened quite suddenly, and for others of us the process was a slower dawning upon our consciousness. However rapidly our spiritual awakening appeared, the path of our spiritual growth varied for all of us. Some of us were agnostics or perhaps even atheists when we first came to the program. Others of us came to this program via other religions. Still others of us had grown up in the church, and thought we knew all about Jesus and spirituality.

Wherever we were when we began this journey, we gradually learned that our true god had been the great, "I" rather than the great "I am." We first had to learn to trust in others, our fellow sojourners, and learn that there exists a power greater than our selves. As we worked the steps, we began to surrender more of ourselves and trust in God. We experienced the difference between religiosity and relationship. Finally, when we opened our hearts to an intimate relationship with the Living God, we experienced a spiritual awakening.

...as the result of these steps...

"But by the grace of God I am what I am, and his grace to me was not without effect. No, I worked harder than all of them – yet not I, but the grace of God that was with me."

– 1 Corinthians 15:10

How many times have we heard someone say, "There, but by the Grace of God, go I"? Paul writes that because of the grace of God he is what he is, that it was God's working in him that changed him from a fanatical Pharisee, capturing and persecuting Christians, into a believer, preaching the very Gospel he tried to extinguish. Paul had been so well known as a persecutor of Christians, that he had to work harder than most of the Apostles to preach the Gospel. Yet he acknowledges even that ability was not his own, but the "...grace of God" that was in him. Some have said that humility is not being convinced of your worthlessness – psychologists call that depression – rather it is recognizing God working within you. By working the 12 Steps we have allowed God to work within us, and we have seen the changes He has wrought.

1. What was it like for you the first time you walked into one of these rooms of sexual addiction recovery? What thoughts and feelings did you experience? _____

_____

2. What was your spirituality like at that time? _____

_____

_____

_____

_____

_____

3. How has your spirituality changed since then? What are the major changes in your spirituality? _____

_____

_____

_____

_____

_____

4. What weaknesses in your spiritual growth do you need to continue to work on? _____

_____

_____

_____

_____

_____

_____

_____

Sharon straightened her stack of notes on the little lectern at the front of the meeting room. She took a deep breath, reminded herself she was NOT going to pass out or die in front of all these people...as long as she kept on breathing. She mustered up a warm smile and tried to find a few familiar faces looking back at her. "Hi, my name is Sharon and I am a Christian in recovery from sexual addiction. I have been sober now for twenty-six months, by the grace of God."

"Hi Sharon!" came the enthusiastic answer from the audience.

"I am here to tonight to share my story with you. My sponsor told me to talk about what it was like for me before I came to program, how God has changed my life through this program, and what it's like now." She took another breath, a sip of water from her glass, and then told her story. She talked about how her life has become so very different than it used to be. She told them how much damage all of her acting out had done to her family, her friends, and to herself. She described the jobs she had lost because of her addiction, and how much it had cost her financially. She even shared about the health issues she developed during her acting out.

When Sharon talked about how God had changed her life she talked about how it was a slow and gradual process; so slow and gradual that she had not realized how very different she had become until she walked into the meeting tonight, and met a newcomer. She shared how it was like looking into a mirror of how she looked the first night she came to program; lost, frightened, hurting, angry, and desperately lonely. She took a moment to thank all the newcomers and told them how they are the most important people in the meeting because they help all of us to remember where we used to be and what it was like. Then she thanked God, because He loved us first, and loved us enough to send His Son, Jesus to die for our sins, that we might be restored to Him. She closed with an encouragement to all of them, "Keep coming back. It works if you work it, and it won't if you don't!"

Everyone broke out into applause and cheers for Sharon. She did not really know what to do so she just grabbed her notes and headed towards the back of the room. It was hard for her to look at the smiling faces as she passed by, but many of them reached to shake her hand or give her a quick hug as she made her way past. "Good job, Sharon!" said one lady whom she recognized but didn't really know. "Thanks Sharon, really good!" said another lady as she passed by.

She changed her mind about sitting down in the back and slipped right on out the door instead. A few more long strides and she rounded the corner and leaned her back against the wall. She didn't know whether she would break out in tears or giggles, but her heart was pounding and she took a few deep breaths to try and calm herself down.

A moment later and she heard Karan's familiar voice, "Sharon? You out here?"

"Yea, I'm here" she replied as she peeked back around the corner. Karan smiled and walked over to join her.

"You know, you were really great in there!" said Karan.

"Really? It's all a blur at the moment," replied Sharon.

"Absolutely!" said Karan. "In fact, I think you are one of the best speakers we've had in quite a while."

"I don't know about that," countered Sharon.

"Well, I do, and I am proud of you. How do you feel?" asked Karan.

"Like I just ran a marathon," laughed Sharon. "I'm exhausted, and exhilarated. I'm scared and feel quite the bit naked having spilled it ALL in front of everyone. Part of me is a bit worried they'll ask me to not come here anymore now that they know how really awful I was."

"Are you kidding!?" exclaimed Karan. "Your story isn't half as bad as most of theirs!" She laughed, "And you tell it twice as good as any of them ever did!"

About then, the noise coming from inside the room began to rise, and people began to come out of the door, many of them clustering in small groups to talk in the fresh, cool air, and a few heading for their cars.

"Ahhmmm, Sharon?" queried a small, thin voice from a group of three young women who had approached.

Sharon turned to find the still skiddish-looking face of Latisha smiling at her. "Hi Latisha," Sharon greeted her.

"Aaahmm...I was wondering if...well, you know people say I need to have a sponsor and all...so I wondered if you would be my sponsor?" Latisha asked meekly.

Sharon glanced at Karan and found her grinning from ear to ear back at her. She looked back at Latisha and said, "You know, Latisha, I would consider it an honor and a privilege. We need to have a talk. Let's find a quiet place to sit down, ok?"

As she walked away she gave one last look back over her shoulder at Karan, and said with emphasis, "Hey GRAND-sponsor! What are you doing standing there!? Get yourself on over here!" and laughed out loud as she turned back around and put her arm around Latisha's shoulder.

...we tried to carry this message...

> "As Jesus was getting into the boat, the man who had been demon-possessed begged to go with him. Jesus did not let him, but said, "Go home to your family and tell them how much the Lord has done for you, and how he has had mercy on you." So the man went away and began to tell in the Decapolis how much Jesus had done for him. And all the people were amazed."
>
> — Mark 5:18 – 20

After Jesus healed the man who had been demon-possessed, he wanted to just hang out with Jesus. Wouldn't you? Jesus, on the other hand, had work for him to do. He sent him home to tell others what God had done for him, to "carry the message" to others who were lost and suffering. We have heard others tell us, "You can only keep it by giving it away."

1. Have you given it away yet? Have you shared the message of your hope in recovery through Jesus Christ? If yes, how did it impact you? _____
_____
_____
_____

2. If you have not shared the message with anyone, why not? _____

3. What is your attitude about volunteering your time for service in program? _____

4. How does practicing the principle of selflessness by serving others impact my ability to stay sober? _____

    By working this simple program we have found not only sobriety, but a spiritual awakening as well.

    Make a list of all the behaviors that are different now versus when you first began the twelve steps. If you need to refresh your memory, go back over your Fourth Step. Share that list with your sponsor and accountability partners.

1. _____
   _____
   _____
2. _____
   _____
   _____
3. _____
   _____
   _____

Go back to your work from Step Three and find the section on "Satan's Lies" and "God's Truths." How are your belief structures different now? How strongly do you still believe those old lies of Satan? How much stronger are you beliefs in God's Truths? Use a 0 – 100% scale where 100% = Completely True and 0% = Not At All.

Satan's Lie   Strength Rating
1. _____
   _____
   _____
2. _____
   _____
   _____
3. _____
   _____
   _____

God's Truth   Strength Rating
1. _____
   _____
   _____
2. _____
   _____
   _____
3. _____
   _____
   _____

What are the different messages that I have to carry to others? _____

_____
_____
_____
_____

You might be wondering, "What can I do to carry the message to others?" Sometimes the most effective mechanisms are indirect. For example, we can volunteer in various service positions in program. Have you ever walked in and been greeted with the aroma of hot coffee? Even before having any contact with a person we know this is a place where we are welcomed. The people who get to the meeting an hour in advance to set up chairs, set out fruit or muffins, and start the coffee percolating send a message of hope by creating a warm and welcoming atmosphere for others. We can carry the message to others in direct ways, such as by sharing our testimony, speaking on panels, or by sponsoring others.

1. In what ways can you attempt to carry the message to others? _____

_____
_____
_____
_____
_____

2. At what times is it difficult for you to share this message with others? (e.g., when I'm struggling, discouraged, attempting to sponsor someone for whom I am not a good match) _____

_____
_____
_____
_____
_____

3. What do you need to do to overcome these difficulties? _____

_____
_____
_____
_____
_____

4. Name three ways that you will try to carry the message to others in the next three months. _____

_____
_____
_____
_____
_____

5. Name one thing you can do this week to carry the message to others: _____

_____
_____
_____
_____
_____

Share that commitment with your sponsor and accountability partners and ask them to hold you to it.

Are you prepared to share your testimony with others? If an opportunity came tomorrow to tell someone of what God has done in your life, would you know what to say? Here are some tips that might be helpful.

1) Take the time to write out your testimony. Share it with your sponsor and accountability partners and ask for their input. Make sure your story highlights these points: what it was like then (before recovery), what its like now, and how God changed your life.

2) Now, convert your long-form testimony into "talking points." Essentially you make an outline that you can memorize the major section headings so that you can talk your way through the major points. That way when the opportunity arises, you have an organized and coherent story to tell.

...to other lust addicts...

> *"There is a destiny that makes us brothers: None goes his way alone;*
> *All that we send into the lives of others comes back onto our own."*
>
> — *Edwin Markham*

At first glance the phrase, "to other lust addicts" seems unnecessary; after all, whom else would we tell? The wisdom of the program tells us that the message of recovery given by an addict is far more powerful than the same message delivered by a non-addict. Could it be a credibility issue? Think of the difference the stories of recovery you heard in these meetings made in your own life. Do you remember the demon-possessed man whom Jesus healed, and then sent him away to tell others? Imagine what it was like for those who heard his testimony. Might they have thought, "Here is he who was crazed and is now restored to his right mind." If Jesus can heal him He can surely heal me!" Your life now serves as a testimony to Jesus' healing power, and He sends you back to the world to share the Good News! Praise God I was a crazed person and am now restored to my right mind!

...and to practice these principles...

> *"Not to go back is somewhat to advance, and men must walk, at least, before they dance."*
>
> — *Alexander Pope*

In our efforts at applying the spiritual principles that the steps teach us, we must first practice the principle of grace to these same efforts. It has been said that addicts have two gears: flat-out and dead-stop. We have to learn that we will struggle, fail, and struggle even more with some of the principles. Take honesty, for example. How many different ways are there to be dishonest? So we begin with small steps and every day strive to be more like Jesus and less like ourselves. Grace gives us the ability to forgive ourselves for our failures and forgiveness allows us to get back up and try again.

You might ask, "What principles? Was there a list? Maybe I was absent that day?" I'm so glad you asked! The principles are simply those we have covered in these twelve steps. Go back through the twelve steps and, in the space provided below, write down at least one principle for each step.

Step One _____

_____

_____

Step Two _____

_____

_____

Step Three _____

_____

_____

Step Four _____

_____

_____

Step Five _____
_____

Step Six _____
_____

Step Seven _____
_____

Step Eight _____
_____

Step Nine _____
_____

Step Ten _____
_____

Step Eleven _____
_____

Step Twelve _____
_____

..in all our affairs.

> "Extremes meet and there is no better example than the haughtiness of humility."
>
> — *Ralph Waldo Emerson*

Being people of extremes, we often compartmentalize our lives, believing that one part of our life has nothing to do with another. Compartmentalization is the mechanism that allowed us to live the secret life of our addiction and at the same time to walk around and look like "normal" people the rest of the day. Compartmentalization, however, is also a numbing of our emotions, a disconnection from our spirituality, and a suspension of our conscience. In recovery, we have to live in one huge room, where our spirituality, emotions, and conscience can all stay connected with one another. Therefore, for example, when we practice honesty with our spouse, with our friends, at work, and in our interactions with strangers, we have practiced the principle of honesty in all our affairs.

1. In what ways do you still struggle with compartmentalization? _____
_____
_____
_____
_____
_____
_____
_____
_____

2. Pick a two or three principles to practice this week and write at least one specific way in which you will practice that principle this week. Repeat these each week until you have mastered them, then replace them with new principles._____
_____
_____
_____
_____
_____
_____
_____
_____
_____
_____
_____
_____
_____
_____

Congratulations, you have completed your first round with the twelve steps. Enjoy the satisfaction of the hard work that you have put into your recovery. Most of us find that while we practice the steps every day, eventually we need to formally work the steps again, and again. Each time we learn something new about others, find an aspect of a spiritual principal we had missed before, or learn something new about ourselves.

Bibliography

Here are some books that have been helpful to us in dealing with the issue of is there a God and Who is He? You can find these online or at your local bookseller.

Spiritual Issues

Josh McDowell	Evidence that Demands a Verdict.
	More Evidence that Demands a Verdict.
	More than a Carpenter.
Jonathan Wells	Icons of Evolution: Science or Myth?
J.I. Packer	Knowing God.
Beth Moore	Believing God
	When Godly People Do UnGodly Things
Neil T. Anderson	The Bondage Breaker
Tyndale House	The Life Recovery Bible
Hazeldon	Answers in the Heart
	(Daily Devotions for Sex Addiction)

Recovery Issues

Patrick Carnes	Out of the Shadows
Steve Gallagher	Out of the Depths of Sexual Sin
Neil Anderson	Released from Bondage
Meg Wilson	Hope After Betrayal
Mark Laaser	Healing the Wounds of Sexual Addiction
	The Pornography Trap

Internet Resources

www.rsaministries.org   www.allaboutgod.com   www.blueletterbible.com

www.swordandspirit.com   www.crosswalk.com

www.cptryon.org/prayer/special/index.html

www.ingramcontent.com/pod-product-compliance
Lightning Source LLC
Chambersburg PA
CBHW051435290426
44109CB00016B/1562